Contents

More TWISTs

18 More Tales that Take a Surprising Turn

With Exercises for Comprehension & Enrichment

by Burton Goodman

JAMESTOWN PUBLISHERS

a division of NTC/CONTEMPORARY PUBLISHING GROUP
Lincolnwood, Illinois USA

TITLES IN THE SERIES

More Twists

Cover and text design: Deborah Hulsey Christie
Cover illustration: Bob Eggleton
Text illustrations: Bob Eggleton: pp. 38, 64, 91, 98, 112, 125
Pamela R. Levy: pp. 24, 32, 45, 57, 105, 118
Thomas Ewing Malloy: pp. 8–9, 17, 51, 70, 78, 84

ISBN: 0-89061-502-0

Published by Jamestown Publishers,
a division of NTC/Contemporary Publishing Group, Inc.,
4255 West Touhy Avenue,
Lincolnwood (Chicago), Illinois 60712-1975 U.S.A.
© 1989, 1993 by Burton Goodman

12 13 14 15 16 17 18 19 20 21 22 100/108 10 09 08 07 06 05 04 03 02 01

To the Student

$\mathcal{T}$his book contains 18 high interest stories of recognized literary merit. As the title suggests, each selection in this volume ends with a *twist*. The stories will provide you with hours of reading pleasure—and the exercises which follow offer a variety of ways to help you improve your reading and literature skills.

You will notice that the exercises have been designed to provide a special *twist* of their own:

> **T**ELLING ABOUT THE STORY
>
> **W**ATCHING FOR NEW VOCABULARY WORDS
>
> **I**DENTIFYING STORY ELEMENTS
>
> **S**ELECTING WORDS FROM THE STORY
>
> **T**HINKING ABOUT THE STORY

There are four questions in each of these exercises. Do all the exercises. Then check your answers with your teacher. Use the scoring chart following each exercise to calculate your score for that exercise. Give yourself 5 points for every correct answer.

Since there are four questions, you can receive up to 20 points for each exercise. Use the TWISTS scoring chart at the end of the exercises to figure your total score. A perfect score for the five exercises would equal 100 points. Keep track of how well you do by recording your score on the Progress Chart on page 133. Then write your score on the Progress Graph on page 134 to plot your progress.

TELLING ABOUT THE STORY will help you improve your reading comprehension skills.

WATCHING FOR NEW VOCABULARY WORDS will help you strengthen your vocabulary skills. Often, you will be able to figure out the meaning of an unfamiliar word by using *context clues*—the words and phrases around the word.

IDENTIFYING STORY ELEMENTS will give you practice in recognizing and understanding the key elements of literature.

SELECTING WORDS FROM THE STORY will help you reinforce both your reading *and* your vocabulary skills through the use of the cloze technique.

THINKING ABOUT THE STORY will help you sharpen your critical thinking skills. You will have opportunities to *reason* by drawing conclusions, making inferences, using story clues, and so forth.

An additional section, **Thinking More About the Story,** offers further opportunities for thoughtful discussion and writing.

On the following page, you will find brief definitions of some important literary terms. If you wish, refer to these definitions when you answer the questions on Identifying Story Elements.

Since there are 18 stories in this collection, you will have the opportunity to read one selection every week of the term, or one selection every other week throughout the school year. Either way, you will enjoy these stories. And the exercises which follow will help you master a number of very important skills.

Now . . . get ready for *More Twists!*

Burton Goodman

The Short Story—Literary Terms

Characterization: the ways a writer shows what a character is like. The way a character acts, speaks, thinks, and looks *characterizes* that person.

Conflict: a struggle or difference of opinion between characters. Sometimes, a character may clash with a force of nature.

Dialogue: the exact words that a character says; usually the conversation between characters.

Foreshadowing: clues which hint or suggest what will happen later in the story.

Inner Conflict: a struggle which takes place in the mind of a character.

Main Character: the person the story is mostly about.

Mood: the feeling or atmosphere that the writer creates. For example, the *mood* of a story might be joyous or suspenseful.

Motive: the reason behind a character's actions.

Narrator: the person who tells the story. Usually, the *narrator* is the writer or a character in the story.

Plot: the series of incidents or happenings in a story. The *plot* is the outline or arrangement of events.

Purpose: the reason the author wrote the story. For example, an author's *purpose* might be to amuse or entertain, to convince, or to inform.

Setting: the time and place of the action in a story; where and when the action takes place.

Style: the way in which a writer uses language. The choice and arrangement of words and sentences help to create the writer's *style*.

Theme: the main, or central idea, of a story.

1. The Interlopers

by Saki

*I*n a forest of tall trees somewhere in Romania, a man stood watching and listening one winter night. You might have thought he was waiting for some beast of the woods to come within range of his sight and his rifle. But the animal he watched for so keenly was not legal or lawful to hunt. No, Ulrich von Gradwitz patrolled the dark forest in search of a *human* enemy.

Gradwitz's forest lands were large and

were well stocked with game. The narrow strip of border land he patrolled was not known for especially good hunting. Still, it was the most carefully guarded of all of Gradwitz's property.

Many years ago, in the days of his grandfather, it had been the subject of a famous lawsuit between the Gradwitzes and a neighboring family. The court ruled that the neighboring family had taken possession of it against the law. The strip of land was returned to the Gradwitzes.

But the neighboring family had never accepted the judgment of the court. Members of the family continually crossed on to Gradwitz's land to hunt. For three generations now there had been bitter feelings between the neighbors.

The feud had grown into a personal one since Ulrich had come to be head of the family. If there was one man he detested and wished ill, it was Georg Znaeym, the head of the neighboring family. As boys, they had thirsted for one another's blood. As men, each hoped that misfortune might fall on the other. And on this wind-filled winter night, Ulrich had banded together his men to patrol the dark forest. They were not searching for four-footed prey. No, they were searching for the prowling thieves he suspected of being on his land that night.

Ulrich strayed away from his men, whom he had placed in ambush on the crest of the hill. He wandered far down the steep slopes through the wild tangle of bushes. He peered through the tree trunks and listened, through the whistling of the wind and the beating of the branches, for sight or sound of the trespassers.

If only on this wild night, in this dark lonely spot, he might come across Georg Znaeym, man to man, with no one to witness it. That was the wish that was first and foremost in his thoughts. And as Ulrich stepped around the trunk of a huge tree, he came face to face with the man he sought.

The two enemies stood glaring at one another for a long silent moment. Each had a rifle in his hand. Each had hate in his heart and murder in his mind. The chance had come to give full play to the passions of a lifetime.

But a man who has been brought up under a civilized code cannot easily bring himself to shoot down his neighbor in cold blood without speaking a word. There was a moment of hesitation before action. And then a deed of Nature's own violence overwhelmed them. There was a flash of lightning following by a splitting crash over their heads. And before they could leap aside, a falling tree had thundered down on them.

Ulrich von Gradwitz found himself stretched on the ground. One arm was numb beneath him and the other was trapped helplessly in a tangle of branches. Both his legs were pinned beneath the fallen mass. His heavy boots had saved his feet from being crushed to pieces. But if his injuries were not as serious as they might have been, it was evident that he could not move from his present position until someone came to release him.

The falling branches had slashed the skin of his face, and he had to wink away some drops of blood from his eyelashes before he could see the scene of the disaster clearly. At his side, so near that, under ordinary circumstances he could almost have touched him, lay Georg Znaeym, alive and struggling. Znaeym was obviously as helplessly pinned down as himself. All around them lay the wreckage of splintered branches and broken twigs.

Ulrich felt relief at being alive. But angered at his helpless plight, he uttered a series of heated shouts. Georg, who was nearly blinded with the blood which trickled across his eyes, stopped his struggling for a moment to listen. Then he gave a short, snarling laugh.

"So, you're not killed as you ought to be. But you're caught anyway," he cried. "Caught fast. Ho, what a joke! Ulrich von Gradwitz trapped in the forest he has stolen! There's real justice for you!"

And he laughed again, mockingly and savagely.

"I'm caught on my *own* forest land," retorted Ulrich. "When my men come to release us you will wish, perhaps, that you were in a better situation than caught hunting illegally on a neighbor's land."

Georg was silent for a moment. Then he answered quietly, "Are you sure that your men will find much to release? I have men, too, in the forest tonight, close behind me. And *they* will be here first to do the releasing. When they drag me out from under these branches, it will be easy to roll this mass of tree trunk over on top of you. Your men will find you dead under a fallen tree. For the sake of form, I shall send a letter of sympathy to your family."

"That is a useful hint," said Ulrich fiercely.

"My men had orders to follow in ten minutes' time, seven of which must have gone by already. And when they get me out, I will remember the hint. Only since you will have met your death hunting unlawfully on my land, I don't think I can send any letter of sympathy to your family."

"Good," snarled Georg. "Good! We fight this quarrel out to the death—you and I and our men, with no one else to come between us. Death to you, Ulrich von Gradwitz."

"The same to you, Georg Znaeym, forest thief. Poacher! Trespasser!"

Both men spoke with the bitterness of possible defeat, for each knew that it might be a long time before his men would seek him out or find him. It was just a matter of chance whose men would arrive first on the scene.

Both had now given up the useless struggle to free themselves from the mass of wood that held them down. Ulrich tried, with difficulty, to bring his one partly free arm close enough to his coat pocket to draw out his wine flask. When he finally accomplished that, it took a long time before he could manage to open the bottle or get any of the liquid down his throat.

It had been a mild winter, and little snow had fallen. Therefore, the captives suffered less from the cold than might have been the case at that time of the year. Still, the wine was warm and reviving to the wounded man. He looked across with something like a throb of pity to where his enemy lay, the groans of pain and weariness coming softly from his lips.

"Could you reach this flask if I threw it over to you?" asked Ulrich suddenly. "There is good wine in it, and one may as well be as comfortable as one can. Let us drink, even if tonight one of us dies."

"No, I can scarcely see anything," said Georg. "There is so much blood caked around my eyes. And in any case, I don't drink wine with an enemy."

Ulrich was silent for a few minutes. He lay listening to the weary howling of the wind. An idea was slowly forming and growing in his brain. It was an idea that gained strength every time that he looked across at the man who was fighting so grimly against pain and exhaustion. In the pain Ulrich himself was feeling, the old fierce hatred seemed to be dying down.

"Neighbor," he said after a while, "do as you please if your men come first. It was a fair agreement. But as for me, I've changed my mind. If my men are the first to arrive you shall be the first to be helped, as though you were my guest. We have quarreled all our lives over this stupid strip of forest land, where the trees can't even stand up straight without falling down in a storm. Lying here tonight, thinking, I've come to realize we've been fools. There are better things in life than getting the better of a boundary dispute. Neighbor, if you will help me to bury the old quarrel I—I will ask you to be my friend."

Georg Znaeym was silent for so long that Ulrich thought he had perhaps fainted from the pain of his injuries. Then Georg spoke slowly.

"How everyone would stare and gossip if we rode into the marketplace together. No one living can remember seeing a Znaeym and a von Gradwitz talking to one another in friendship. What peace there would be if we ended our feud tonight. And if we choose to make peace among our people, who could interfere? No one. There would be no one to interfere—no interlopers from outside.

"You would come to my house and be my guest. And I would be a guest at your castle. I would never fire a shot on your land except when you invited me as a guest. And you would come and hunt with me down in the marshes where the wild fowl are. In all the countryside there is no one who could prevent it if we decided to make peace. I never thought to have wanted to do other than hate you all my life. But I think I have changed my mind about things too, this last half hour. And you offered me your wine flask. Ulrich von Gradwitz, I will be your friend."

For a while both men were silent, turning over in their minds the wonderful changes that this sudden new friendship would bring about.

In the cold, gloomy forest, the wind tore in gusts through the branches and around the tree trunks. The men lay and waited for the help that would now bring release and relief to both of them. And each silently hoped that his men might be the first to arrive, so that he might be the first to show attention to the enemy that had become a friend.

Soon the wind dropped for a moment, and Ulrich broke the silence.

"Let's shout for help," he said. "In this calm, our voices may carry for some distance."

"They won't carry very far through the trees and bushes," said Georg. "But we can try. Together then."

The two raised their voices in a loud call.

"Together again," said Ulrich a few minutes later, after listening in vain for an answering call.

"I heard something that time, I think," said Ulrich.

"I heard nothing but the howling wind," said Georg, hoarsely.

There was silence again for some minutes. Then Ulrich gave a joyful cry.

"I can see figures coming through the woods. They are following the path I took down the hillside."

Both men raised their voices in as loud a shout as they could manage.

"They hear us! They've stopped. Now they see us. They're running down the hill toward us," cried Ulrich.

"How many of them are there?" asked Georg.

"I can't see clearly," said Ulrich. "Nine or ten."

"Then they are yours," said Georg. "I had only seven men with me."

"They are making all the speed they can, brave lads," said Ulrich happily.

"Are they your men?" asked Georg. "Are they your men?" he repeated again as Ulrich did not answer.

"No," said Ulrich with a laugh, the wild laugh of a man filled with hideous fear.

"Who are they?" asked Georg quickly, straining his eyes to see what the other would gladly not have seen.

Wolves.

TELLING ABOUT THE STORY. Complete each of the following statements by putting an *x* in the box next to the correct answer. Each statement tells something about the story.

1. Ulrich von Gradwitz and Georg Znaeym were
   - ☐ a. old friends who enjoyed hunting together.
   - ☐ b. enemies who had feuded for many years.
   - ☐ c. partners who owned a piece of land.

2. Georg could not move because he
   - ☐ a. had promised to wait at that spot for his men.
   - ☐ b. was pinned under a mass of wood.
   - ☐ c. was so shocked at seeing Ulrich.

3. Ulrich offered Georg
   - ☐ a. some wine.
   - ☐ b. bandages for his cuts.
   - ☐ c. part of his land.

4. At the end of the story, the figures which headed toward Georg and Ulrich were
   - ☐ a. Georg's men.
   - ☐ b. Ulrich's men.
   - ☐ c. wolves.

WATCHING FOR NEW VOCABULARY WORDS. Answer the following vocabulary questions by putting an *x* in the box next to the correct response.

1. If there was one man Ulrich detested and wished ill, it was Georg Znaeym. What is the meaning of the word *detested*?
   - ☐ a. hated
   - ☐ b. admired
   - ☐ c. trusted

2. Ulrich's first and foremost wish was to find Georg Znaeym. The word *foremost* means
   - ☐ a. most important.
   - ☐ b. least important.
   - ☐ c. saddest.

3. When the enemies met, they had a chance to "give full play to the passions of a lifetime." Define the word *passions*.
   - ☐ a. pleasant thoughts
   - ☐ b. great hopes
   - ☐ c. strong feelings

4. When he realized he was trapped under the tree, Ulrich was angered by his helpless plight. What is the meaning of the word *plight*?
   - ☐ a. good luck
   - ☐ b. bad situation
   - ☐ c. old injury

☐ × 5 = ☐
NUMBER CORRECT   YOUR SCORE

☐ × 5 = ☐
NUMBER CORRECT   YOUR SCORE

IDENTIFYING STORY ELEMENTS. Each of the following questions tests your understanding of story elements. Put an x in the box next to each correct answer.

1. What is the *setting* of "The Interlopers"?
   ☐ a. a forest in Romania
   ☐ b. a castle in a heavily wooded area
   ☐ c. a plain somewhere in Germany

2. Which statement best *characterizes* Ulrich?
   ☐ a. He was not able to feel any pity to an enemy.
   ☐ b. When he saw his enemy, helpless and hurt, he began to pity him.
   ☐ c. He had always pitied Georg Znaeym.

3. What happened last in the *plot* of the story?
   ☐ a. A tree came crashing down on Georg and Ulrich.
   ☐ b. Georg and Ulrich agreed to be friends.
   ☐ c. Ulrich saw nine or ten figures heading toward them.

4. Identify the sentence which best expresses the *theme* of this story.
   ☐ a. Life is too short to hold foolish grudges.
   ☐ b. One should always try to gain revenge on an enemy.
   ☐ c. It can be very dangerous to hunt alone in a forest.

SELECTING WORDS FROM THE STORY. Complete the following paragraph by filling in each blank with one of the words listed below. Each of the words appears in the story. Since there are five words and four blanks, one word in the group will not be used.

Wolves are _____ animals that
1

look like large dogs. Many people

_____ wolves. However, wolves
2

almost never attack _____ beings.
3

Wolves live and hunt in family units called

packs. Each pack works together to surround

and pull down its _____ . Wolves
4

may be found in North America, Europe,

Greenland, and Asia.

human   wild

tree

prey   fear

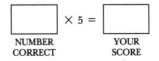

NUMBER CORRECT × 5 = YOUR SCORE

NUMBER CORRECT × 5 = YOUR SCORE

THINKING ABOUT THE STORY. Each of the following questions requires you to think critically about the selection. Put an *x* in the box next to the correct answer.

1. We may infer that Georg and Ulrich were
   ☐ a. ignored by the wolves.
   ☐ b. saved at the last moment.
   ☐ c. killed by wild animals.

2. This story suggests that Georg and Ulrich
   ☐ a. had very little in common.
   ☐ b. wasted many years during which they might have been friends.
   ☐ c. should have continued their quarrel.

3. If Georg's men had arrived first, they would probably have
   ☐ a. rolled a tree trunk over Ulrich.
   ☐ b. helped Ulrich to safety.
   ☐ c. left Ulrich to die.

4. What point does this story make?
   ☐ a. It is hard to remain the enemy of a person who has shown you kindness.
   ☐ b. Neighbors should always be the best of friends.
   ☐ c. It is impossible for people to change.

☐ × 5 = ☐
NUMBER   YOUR
CORRECT   SCORE

Thinking More About the Story

● Georg said that if he and Ulrich decided to make peace, there would be no one to interfere—"no interlopers from outside." Who were "the interlopers" in this story? Do you think it is a good title for the selection? Explain.

● Suppose that Georg and Ulrich were saved at the last moment. Do you think they would have become good friends? Or would they eventually have become enemies again? Explain your answer.

● If the tree had not fallen when it did, trapping Georg and Ulrich, how do you think the story would have ended? Give reasons to support your answer.

Use the boxes below to total your scores for the exercises.

☐
+
Telling About the Story

☐
+
Watching for New Vocabulary Words

☐
+
Identifying Story Elements

☐
+
Selecting Words from the Story

☐
▼
Thinking About the Story

☐
Score Total: Story 1

16

2. The Last Leaf

by O. Henry

*I*n New York City, you may find an old section which is known as Greenwich Village. There, on streets which run this way and that at unusual and unpredictable angles, live many artists.

On the top floor of a three-story brick building Sue and Joanna had their studio. One was from Maine, the other from California. They had met at a coffee shop on Eighth Street, and found their tastes in art and food and clothing so similar, they decided to rent a studio together.

That was in May some years ago. In November, a cold, unseen stranger whom the doctors called Pneumonia, stalked about the city touching one victim here and another there with his icy fingers.

Joanna he smote, and she lay, scarcely moving, on her bed, looking through the small window at the brick wall of the adjoining building.

One morning the doctor beckoned Sue

into the hallway. Shaking his head and raising his shaggy eyebrows, he said, "Joanna has one chance in, let us say ten. And that chance is for her to *want* to live. In cases like this, the will to survive is everything. But I'm afraid that Joanna has made up her mind that she's not going to get well."

The doctor paused for a moment. "Tell me," he said, "isn't there something special she has to live for—something worth fighting for to get well?"

"Well," said Sue, "she once spoke about traveling to Italy. She wants to paint a picture of the Bay of Naples some day."

"*Some* day, *ha!*" scoffed the doctor. "Hasn't she anything worth fighting for right now?"

"Nothing I can think of, doctor."

"Well," said the doctor, "there is just so much that science can accomplish. Make certain that Joanna takes this medicine. Still, if you could find something to make her *want* to live, you would increase her chances a hundred percent."

After the doctor had gone, Sue went into Joanna's room. Joanna lay, scarcely moving, with her face toward the window. Her eyes were wide open. She was looking out the window and counting—counting backward.

"Twelve," she said. And a little later "eleven"; and then "ten," and "nine"; and then "eight" and "seven" almost together.

Sue looked out of the window. What was there to count? There was only a bare, dreary yard to be seen—and the side of the brick house twenty feet away. An old, decaying ivy vine, twisted and gnarled, climbed halfway up the brick wall. The autumn winds had blown the leaves from the vine so that it clung, thin and almost bare, against the bricks.

"What is it?" asked Sue.

"Six," said Joanna, almost in a whisper. "They're falling faster now. Three days ago there were almost a hundred. It made my head ache to count them. But now it's easy. There goes another one. There are only five left now."

"Five what, Joanna? What are you counting?"

"Leaves. On the ivy vine. When the last one falls I must go, too. I've known that for three days. Didn't the doctor tell you?"

"I never heard such nonsense," complained Sue, with a show of scorn. "What have old ivy leaves got to do with your getting well? Why the doctor just told me that your chances for getting well soon were—let's see, exactly what did he say? He said the odds were ten to one! Have a bite now to keep up your strength. I'll get you some soup. Then I must get back to my work, for there are some illustrations I've got to finish."

"There goes another leaf," said Joanna, keeping her eyes on the window. "No, I don't want any soup. That leaves just four. I want to see the last one fall before it gets dark. Then I'll go, too."

"Joanna," said Sue, "will you promise me to keep your eyes closed and not look out the window until I am finished working? I must hand those illustrations in by tomorrow. I need the light, or I would pull the shade down."

"Couldn't you draw in the other room?" asked Joanna.

"I want to keep an eye on you," said Sue.

"Besides, I don't want you to continue looking at those silly ivy leaves."

"Tell me as soon as you have finished," said Joanna, closing her eyes, and lying as still as a fallen statue. "I want to see the last leaf fall. I'm tired of waiting. I'm tired of thinking. I want to turn loose my hold on everything, and go sailing down, down, down, just like one of those poor, tired leaves."

"Try to sleep," said Sue. "I want to speak to Mr. Behrman downstairs about being the model for the illustration of a miner I'm drawing. I'll only be gone a few minutes. Don't try to move until I get back."

Mr. Behrman was a painter who lived on the ground floor beneath them. Well past sixty with a long curly beard, he was a failure in art. For forty years, he had always been just about to paint a masterpiece—but he had never yet begun it. For several years he had done no painting except for odds and ends advertising jobs which he found now and then. He earned a little money by working as a model for young artists in the area. To many, he was a fierce little old man who talked often of his coming masterpiece. But he regarded himself as the special protector of the two young artists in the studio above.

Sue found Behrman sitting in a corner of his dimly lighted den below. In one corner was a blank canvas on an easel that, for twenty-five years, he had been waiting there for the first brush strokes of the masterpiece.

Sue told Behrman of Joanna's fancy, and explained how she feared that Joanna, light and fragile as a leaf herself, would, indeed, float away when her slight hold upon the world grew weaker.

Old Behrman, his eyes glaring, shouted his contempt for such silly imaginings.

"What!" he cried. "Are there people in the world foolish enough to die because leaves drop from a vine? I have not heard of such a thing. Why do you allow such nonsense to fill that brain of hers?"

"She is very ill and weak," said Sue, "and the fever has affected her."

"It is this chilly house which has made her sick," said Behrman. "Some day I will paint a masterpiece. Then you shall have enough money to take a vacation in some sunny place."

Joanna was sleeping when they went upstairs. Sue pulled the shade down to the window sill, and motioned Behrman into the other room. In there, they fearfully peered out the window toward the ivy vine. A cold rain mingled with snow was falling. For a moment they looked at each other without speaking. Then Behrman, in his old blue shirt, took a seat and assumed the look of a miner.

When Sue awoke from a two hours' sleep the next morning, she found Joanna, with dull, wide-open eyes, staring at the window shade.

"Pull the shade up," she ordered in a whisper. "I want to see."

Wearily, Sue obeyed.

Sue stared, amazed. After a night of beating rain and fierce gusts of wind, one ivy leaf still stood out against the brick wall. It was the last one on the vine. Still dark green near its stem, but with its edges tinted with a failing yellow, it hung bravely from a branch some twenty feet above the ground.

"It is the last leaf," said Joanna. "I thought it would surely fall during the night. I heard the wind. It will fall today, and I shall die at the same time."

"Joanna, please don't talk that way. Think of me if you won't think of yourself. What would I do?"

But Joanna did not answer. The day wore on, and through the twilight they could see the lone ivy leaf clinging to its stem against the wall. At night, it started to rain again. The wind whistled sharply. Sue pulled down the shade.

When morning came, Joanna asked that the shade be raised.

The ivy leaf was still there.

For a long time, Joanna lay staring at it. And then she called to Sue who was in the other room. "I've been wrong, Sue," said Joanna. "Something has made that last leaf stay there to show me how wicked I was. It's a sin to want to die. Please bring me some breakfast now. No, first put some pillows behind my back, and bring me today's newspaper when you can."

An hour later she said, "Sue, I know that some day I'm going to paint the Bay of Naples."

The doctor came in the afternoon, and paused to speak to Sue in the hallway as he left. "She has an even chance," he said. "Give her good care and you'll win. And now I must see another case I have downstairs. His name is Behrman—some kind of an artist, I believe. He has pneumonia, too. He is elderly and weak and the ailment is severe. There is no hope for him. But he goes to the hospital today to be made more comfortable."

The next day the doctor said to Sue, "Joanna's out of danger now. You've won. Proper food and rest—that's all she needs."

That afternoon, Sue came to the bedroom where she found Joanna sitting up, drawing.

"I have something to tell you," Sue said. "Mr. Behrman died of pneumonia in the hospital today. He was ill just two days. On the morning of the first day, a neighbor found him in his room downstairs helpless with pain. His shoes and clothing were drenched with rain, and icy cold. They couldn't imagine where he had been on such a dreadful night."

Shocked, Joanna stared at her friend.

"And then," said Sue, "they found a lantern, still lighted. And a ladder that had been dragged from its place. And some scattered brushes, and tubes with green and yellow colors. Look out the window at the last ivy leaf on the wall. Didn't you wonder why it never fluttered or moved when the wind blew? Oh, Joanna, it's Behrman's masterpiece—he painted it there the night that the last leaf fell."

TELLING ABOUT THE STORY. Complete each of the following statements by putting an *x* in the box next to the correct answer. Each statement tells something about the story.

1. Joanna was ill with
   □ a. a bad cold.
   □ b. pneumonia.
   □ c. an illness the doctor could not identify.

2. When Joanna looked out of her window, she saw a
   □ a. row of houses.
   □ b. large tree with hundreds of leaves.
   □ c. vine climbing up a brick wall.

3. At the end of the story, the doctor said that
   □ a. it was necessary for Joanna to go to the hospital.
   □ b. there was no hope for Joanna.
   □ c. Joanna was out of danger.

4. A neighbor found Mr. Behrman
   □ a. in pain and drenched from the rain.
   □ b. staring sadly at a blank canvas.
   □ c. painting a leaf on the wall.

WATCHING FOR NEW VOCABULARY WORDS. Answer the following vocabulary questions by putting an *x* in the box next to the correct response.

1. The old vine was twisted and gnarled. What is the meaning of the word *gnarled*?
   □ a. knotted
   □ b. straight
   □ c. green

2. Behrman, eyes glaring, showed his contempt for such silly ideas. Define the word *contempt*.
   □ a. pleasure
   □ b. hope
   □ c. scorn

3. Not far away was the brick wall of the adjoining building. The word *adjoining* means
   □ a. beautiful.
   □ b. neighboring.
   □ c. aged.

4. The doctor said that Mr. Behrman's ailment was severe. What is the meaning of the word *ailment*?
   □ a. talent
   □ b. experience
   □ c. illness

[ ] × 5 = [ ]

NUMBER CORRECT   YOUR SCORE

[ ] × 5 = [ ]

NUMBER CORRECT   YOUR SCORE

IDENTIFYING STORY ELEMENTS. Each of the following questions tests your understanding of story elements. Put an *x* in the box next to each correct answer.

1. What is the *setting* of "The Last Leaf"?
   - ☐ a. a doctor's office in New York City
   - ☐ b. an apartment in Greenwich Village
   - ☐ c. an artist's studio in California

2. What happened first in the *plot* of the story?
   - ☐ a. The doctor said that Joanna's chances were one in ten.
   - ☐ b. Sue told Mr. Behrman about Joanna's illness.
   - ☐ c. Joanna asked Sue to bring her a newspaper.

3. Which sentence best *characterizes* Mr. Behrman?
   - ☐ a. He cared for nothing but his work.
   - ☐ b. He was willing to make a sacrifice for Joanna.
   - ☐ c. He could have earned a great deal of money painting masterpieces.

4. Identify the statement which best expresses one *theme* of this story.
   - ☐ a. It is necessary for all young artists to suffer.
   - ☐ b. If you stay out-of-doors at night in a storm, you are likely to get sick.
   - ☐ c. Sometimes, the will to live can be a powerful medicine.

	× 5 =	
NUMBER CORRECT		YOUR SCORE

SELECTING WORDS FROM THE STORY. Complete the following paragraph by filling in each blank with one of the words listed below. Each of the words appears in the story. Since there are five words and four blanks, one word in the group will not be used.

Greenwich Village has always

_____ to painters, musicians,
         1

actors, and others interested in the arts. You

will enjoy a stroll _____ this
                  2

interesting and exciting neighborhood.

Tourists and _____ walk along
                 3

the narrow streets. Here you will find

sidewalk cafés and art galleries, as well as

clothing _____ , bakeries, and book
              4

stores. No visit to New York City would be

complete without a trip to Greenwich Village.

shops   beckoned

through

artists   autumn

	× 5 =	
NUMBER CORRECT		YOUR SCORE

THINKING ABOUT THE STORY. Each of the following questions requires you to think critically about the selection. Put an *x* in the box next to the correct answer.

1. We may infer that Behrman's masterpiece was a
   □ a. picture he created for an advertising agency.
   □ b. life-like leaf painted on a wall.
   □ c. painting of the Bay of Naples.

2. Which statement is probably true?
   □ a. If Behrman had lived, he would have become a famous painter.
   □ b. Sue was really not very concerned about Joanna.
   □ c. Behrman saved Joanna's life.

3. This story suggests that the last leaf
   □ a. was not as beautiful as the other leaves.
   □ b. was just about to fall.
   □ c. taught Joanna an important lesson.

4. Which of the following indicates that Joanna was on the road to recovery?
   □ a. She asked for breakfast and a newspaper.
   □ b. She looked out of the window and began counting backward.
   □ c. She wanted to see the last leaf fall.

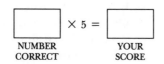

NUMBER CORRECT   × 5 =   YOUR SCORE

Thinking More About the Story

- In saving Joanna's life, Mr. Behrman gave up his own. Was Mr. Behrman a hero—or was he foolish? Explain your answer.
- There is an expression which states that "Opposites attract." Does this apply in the case of Joanna and Sue? Support your answer by showing how they were different or alike.
- Toward the end of the story, Joanna stated, "I know that some day I'm going to paint the Bay of Naples." At this point, we can be quite sure that Joanna is going to live. Why?

Use the boxes below to total your scores for the exercises.

☐ **T**elling About the Story
+
☐ **W**atching for New Vocabulary Words
+
☐ **I**dentifying Story Elements
+
☐ **S**electing Words from the Story
+
☐ **T**hinking About the Story
▼
☐ **S**core Total: Story 2

23

3. The Necklace

by Guy de Maupassant

*M*athilde was a pretty and charming young woman. But, as if by some mistake of fate, she was born into a family which was quite poor. She had no money and no hope for obtaining it. She had no way of becoming known in society. She had no chance to meet and marry a rich and famous man. So she married a clerk in the Department of Education.

She dressed plainly because she could not afford to dress well. This bothered her very much and made her unhappy. She acted as though she were once very wealthy and had lost all her money.

She suffered all the time because she believed that she was born for luxuries. She suffered because of the poverty of her apartment. The walls were dirty. The chairs were worn out. The curtains were ugly. Someone else might not have minded these things so much. But they tortured her and made her angry. She dreamed of servants, of dinners by candlelight, of sitting in large rooms talking with well-known and influential friends.

When she sat down to dinner, her husband would lift the lid on the pot.

"Ah. Good stew!" he would say. "There's nothing I like better than that."

And she would think of magnificent dinners, of expensive plates, of shining silverware.

She had no fine dresses, no jewels—nothing. And she loved things like those. She felt made for them. She would so have liked to please. She wanted to be envied, to be charming, to be popular.

She had a friend, Madame Forestier, a former schoolmate, who was rich. Mathilde did not see her very often, because she suffered so much when she came back to her own drab apartment.

But, one evening, her husband came home looking very pleased. He held a large envelope in his hand.

"Here," he said. "I've got something for you."

She quickly tore open the envelope. Inside was a printed card with these words:

The Minister of Public Education
requests the honor of your presence
at the Annual Ball of the Department
of Education on Friday evening, January 18th.

Instead of being delighted, she threw the invitation on the table. "What do you want me to do with that?" she murmured.

"But, my dear, I thought you would be glad. You never go out, and this is such a good opportunity. I had an awful lot of trouble getting it. Everyone wants to go, and not many members of the office staff have been invited. You'll see all the most important people in Paris there."

She looked at him, annoyed. "And what do you want me to wear?" she asked impatiently.

He had not thought of that. "He stammered, "Why, the dress you always go out in. That looks quite nice, I think."

He stopped, seeing that his wife was crying. "What's the matter?" he asked. "What's the trouble?"

Finally, she gained control of herself. "Nothing," she replied in a calm voice. "Only I have no dress to wear. Therefore I can't go to this ball. Give your card to some friend whose wife has better clothes than I."

He was in despair. "Let's see, Mathilde," he said. "How much would a suitable dress cost? Something very simple which you could wear on other occasions?"

She thought for several seconds. She wondered how much she could ask for without getting a quick refusal from her thrifty husband.

Finally, she answered, "I don't know exactly. But I think I could manage it with four hundred francs."

He grew pale. Four hundred francs was just the amount he had set aside to buy a rifle so that he could go hunting with some friends next summer.

However, he said, "All right. I'll give you four hundred francs. But be sure to buy a pretty dress."

The day of the ball drew near. Mathilde Loisel seemed sad, uneasy, anxious. Her dress was ready, however. Her husband said to her one evening:

"What's the matter, Mathilde? You've been so quiet these last three days."

"It annoys me," she answered, "not to have a single jewel. Not one stone to put on. I'll look so out of place. I'd almost rather not go at all."

"You might wear some flowers," he

suggested. "They're in style this time of year. For ten francs you can get two or three beautiful roses."

She was not convinced. "No," she said, "there's nothing worse than looking poor among other woman who are rich."

"Wait!" he cried. "Go see your friend Madame Forestier, and ask her to lend you some jewels. You know each other well enough for you to do that."

"Why, that's true!" she said, happily. "I hadn't thought of that."

The next day she went to her friend and explained her problem.

Madame Forestier went to a closet, took out a large jewel box, and opened it.

"Pick something out, my dear," Madame Forestier said.

First Mathilde saw some bracelets, then a pearl necklace, then some gold pieces, and some marvelous gems. She tried on the jewelry in front of the mirror. Everything looked so beautiful that she couldn't make up her mind. She kept on asking, "Have you any more?"

"Oh, yes, keep on looking. I don't know what you like."

All of a sudden Mathilde found, in a black satin box, a superb diamond necklace. Her hands trembled as she picked it up. She fastened it around her throat and stared, with delight, at her reflection in the mirror.

She asked breathlessly, "Can you lend me this. Only this?"

"Why, yes, certainly."

Elated, Mathilde kissed her friend with joy. Then she fled with her treasure.

The day of the ball arrived. Mathilde Loisel was a great success. She was the prettiest one there. She was gracious, smiling, and charming. Important men asked who she was, asked to be introduced, asked for a chance to dance with her. And she danced and danced, filled with pleasure. She danced madly, in a kind of cloud of happiness. She danced with the knowledge that she had been a complete success.

When the ball ended, it was very late. "Wait a bit," her husband said. "You'll catch cold outside. I'll go and call a cab."

But she did not listen. They rapidly descended the stairs. But when they got to the street, they couldn't find a cab. Shivering with cold, they finally found one after some time.

The cab dropped them at their door, and they sadly climbed up the stairs. It was all over for her. And as for him, he groaned that he had to be at work at ten o'clock in the morning.

She removed the coat in front of the mirror. She wanted to take one last look at herself. Then suddenly she cried out. She no longer had the necklace around her neck!

"What's the matter?" said her husband.

She turned wildly towards him. "I have—I have—I've lost Madame Forestier's necklace."

He stood up, alarmed.

"What? How? Impossible!"

And they looked in the folds of her dress, in the folds of her coat. In her pockets. Everywhere. They did not find it.

He asked, "You're sure you had it on when you left the ball?"

"Yes. I felt it when we came down the stairs."

"But if you had lost it in the street, we would have heard it fall. You must have lost it in the cab."

"Yes, probably. Did you notice the number?"

"No. And you?"

"No."

They looked at one another, horrified.

"I'll go back on foot," he said. "I'll go over the whole route we took, and see if I can find it."

And he went out. She sat waiting on a chair in her ball dress. She didn't have the strength to go to bed.

Her husband came back about seven o'clock. He had found nothing.

He went to Police Headquarters. He went to the newspaper offices to offer a reward. He went to the cab companies.

She waited all day, mad with fear.

Loisel returned at night. His face was hollow and pale. He had discovered nothing.

"You must write to your friend," he said. "Tell her that you have broken the lock on the necklace and that you are having it repaired. That will at least give us a little time."

She wrote as he suggested.

At the end of the week they had lost all hope. Loisel, who had aged five years during this time, declared:

"We must figure out how to replace that necklace."

The next day they took the case which had held the necklace, and they went to the jeweler whose name was written inside. He looked through his records.

"It was not I who sold that necklace," the jeweler said. "I only supplied the case."

Then they went from jeweler to jeweler, searching for a necklace just like the other one. They were both sick with worry and despair. Finally, they found a diamond necklace that seemed exactly like the one they were seeking. At least it seemed identical. It was priced at forty thousand francs. The jeweler said they could have it for thirty-six thousand.

So they begged the jeweler not to sell it for three days. And they agreed that he would buy it back for thirty-four thousand francs if they found the other one before the end of February.

Loisel had a little money that his father had left him. He would borrow the rest.

He did borrow. He asked for a thousand francs here, five hundred francs there. He signed notes, made promises, agreed to terrible deals. He took chances without being certain that he could ever pay back the money. Finally, after three miserable days, he was able to place the thirty-six thousand francs on the jeweler's counter.

Mathilde immediately took the necklace to her friend. Madame Forestier said to her coldly, "You should have returned it sooner. I might have needed it."

Fortunately, Madame Forestier did not open the case, as her friend had feared. If she had noticed the difference, what would she have thought? What would she have said? Would she have taken Madame Loisel for a thief?

Madame Loisel now began to know the horrible existence of the needy. That terrible debt had to be paid. She would help pay it. They moved out of their apartment and rented a tiny attic under a roof.

She came to know what heavy housework meant. She washed dishes, using her rosy nails on the pots and pans. She scrubbed dirty clothes which she later hung on a line to dry. She carried out garbage. She went shopping, bargained for everything, insulted shopkeepers.

Each month they had to pay some debts. Others they managed to postpone, gaining more time.

Her husband worked evenings doing all kinds of bookkeeping. Then late at night, he copied manuscripts to earn a few extra francs.

And this life lasted ten years.

At the end of ten years they had paid back everything. Everything—the money as well as the high interest on it.

Madame Loisel looked old now. Her hair was messy and her hands were red. She had become rough and hard. She talked loudly while she washed floors with a bucket of water. But sometimes, while her husband was at work, she would sit near the window and think of that evening long ago, of that ball where she had been so beautiful and admired.

What would have happened if she had not lost that necklace? Who knows? Who can say? Life is strange and filled with changes. How little a thing is needed for us to be lost or be saved.

One Sunday Madame Loisel wanted to take a break from her hard week's labors. She decided to take a walk along the wide and beautiful avenue Champs Élysées. Suddenly, she noticed a woman walking with a child. It was Madame Forestier, still young, still beautiful, still charming.

Madame Loisel felt moved. Should she speak to her? Of course. Now that she had paid for the necklace, she would tell her the whole story. Why not?

She went up to her. "Hello, Jeanne," said Mathilde Loisel.

The other was astonished at hearing her first name being called by a common stranger. She did not recognize Mathilde, and stammered:

"But—I do not know you—You must be mistaken."

"No. I am Mathilde Loisel."

Her friend cried out, "Oh, my poor Mathilde! How you have changed!"

"Yes, I've had hard times since I last saw you. Wretched days—and all because of you."

"Because of me? What do you mean?"

"Do you remember that diamond necklace you once lent me?"

"Yes. Well?"

"Well, I lost it."

"What do you mean? You brought it back."

"I brought you back another just like it. And we've been paying for it for ten years now. You can understand that it was not very easy for us who had nothing. Well, it's over now, and I am very glad."

Madame Forestier stopped short.

"You say that you bought a diamond necklace to replace mine?"

"Yes. You never noticed it, then! They were very much alike."

And Madame Loisel smiled proudly.

Madame Forestier, deeply moved, took her friend's hands in her own.

"Oh, my poor Mathilde," she said. "My necklace was made of glass—a fake. At most it was worth only 500 francs!"

TELLING ABOUT THE STORY. Complete each of the following statements by putting an *x* in the box next to the correct answer. Each statement tells something about the story.

1. Mathilde said that she could not go to the ball because she didn't
   - ☐ a. have an invitation.
   - ☐ b. have a dress to wear.
   - ☐ c. know anyone who would be there.

2. At the ball, Mathilde was
   - ☐ a. a great success.
   - ☐ b. too shy to dance.
   - ☐ c. hardly noticed by anyone.

3. When Mathilde arrived home after the ball, she discovered that
   - ☐ a. someone had sent her flowers.
   - ☐ b. the lock on the necklace needed to be repaired.
   - ☐ c. she had lost the necklace.

4. Madame Forestier told Mathilde that the diamond necklace
   - ☐ a. was very valuable.
   - ☐ b. was made of glass.
   - ☐ c. had been in her family for years.

WATCHING FOR NEW VOCABULARY WORDS. Answer the following vocabulary questions by putting an *x* in the box next to the correct response.

1. Mathilde suffered very much because her apartment was so drab. What is the meaning of the word *drab*?
   - ☐ a. large
   - ☐ b. dull
   - ☐ c. expensive

2. She was so elated, Mathilde kissed her friend with joy. The word *elated* means
   - ☐ a. delighted.
   - ☐ b. worried.
   - ☐ c. undecided.

3. The Loisels were looking for a necklace that was identical to the one that had been lost. Which expression best defines the word *identical*?
   - ☐ a. as expensive as
   - ☐ b. as long as
   - ☐ c. exactly the same as

4. Each month they managed to postpone some debts, gaining more time. What is the meaning of the word *postpone*?
   - ☐ a. ask questions about
   - ☐ b. put off until later
   - ☐ c. send by mail

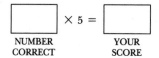

☐	× 5 =	☐
NUMBER CORRECT		YOUR SCORE

☐	× 5 =	☐
NUMBER CORRECT		YOUR SCORE

IDENTIFYING STORY ELEMENTS. Each of the following questions tests your understanding of story elements. Put an *x* in the box next to each correct answer.

1. What happened first in the *plot* of "The Necklace"?
   □ a. Mathilde met Madame Forestier who was walking with a child.
   □ b. Mr. Loisel gave his wife an invitation to a ball.
   □ c. The Loisels went from jeweler to jeweler, searching for a necklace.

2. Which statement best *characterizes* Mathilde?
   □ a. She often spent time with rich and famous people.
   □ b. She was happy because she had fine clothing and jewelry.
   □ c. She was unhappy because she felt she deserved luxuries.

3. What was Mathilde's *motive* for visiting Madame Forestier?
   □ a. She wanted to borrow some jewelry.
   □ b. She wanted to borrow money for a dress.
   □ c. She wanted to talk about their old school days.

4. The *mood* of "The Necklace" is
   □ a. humorous and amusing.
   □ b. sad and serious.
   □ c. happy or joyous.

	× 5 =	
NUMBER CORRECT		YOUR SCORE

SELECTING WORDS FROM THE STORY. Complete the following paragraph by filling in each blank with one of the words listed below. Each of the words appears in the story. Since there are five words and four blanks, one word in the group will not be used.

Diamonds are among the rarest and most _____ of all gems. Often, these beautiful _____ are set into engagement and wedding rings. But diamonds are also used widely in industry. Because they are extremely hard, diamonds are very _____ for cutting and grinding metals. In fact, most of the diamonds mined today _____ up as tools rather than as jewels.

stones   debts

expensive

end   suitable

	× 5 =	
NUMBER CORRECT		YOUR SCORE

THINKING ABOUT THE STORY. Each of the following questions requires you to think critically about the selection. Put an *x* in the box next to the correct answer.

1. We may infer that "The Necklace" takes place in
   □ a. the United States.
   □ b. England.
   □ c. France.

2. Clues in the story suggest that Mathilde often felt
   □ a. satisfied with her life.
   □ b. jealous of others.
   □ c. very proud of her husband.

3. When Madame Forestier learned that the Loisels had been paying for the necklace for ten years, she was probably
   □ a. pleased.
   □ b. honored.
   □ c. shocked.

4. The author seems to suggest that
   □ a. a single incident can sometimes change the entire course of a person's life.
   □ b. wealthy people are almost always greedy.
   □ c. everyone should have beautiful and expensive jewelry.

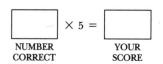

NUMBER
CORRECT   × 5 =   YOUR
                      SCORE

Thinking More About the Story

- How did Mathilde Loisel change during the course of the story? Be sure to describe her strengths and weaknesses in your answer.
- Mathilde might have told Madame Forestier that she had lost the necklace and was planning to replace it. Instead, she decided to purchase a new necklace without informing her friend. Why do you think she decided to do this?
- Suppose Mathilde had told Madame Forestier that she intended to replace the necklace. How would this have changed the course of Mathilde's life?

Use the boxes below to total your scores for the exercises.

☐ Telling About the Story
+
☐ Watching for New Vocabulary Words
+
☐ Identifying Story Elements
+
☐ Selecting Words from the Story
+
☐ Thinking About the Story
▼
☐ Score Total: Story 3

31

4. Appointment with Love

by S. I. Kishor

Six minutes to six, said the great round clock over the information booth in Grand Central Station. The tall young army lieutenant who had just come from the direction of the tracks lifted his sunburned face. His eyes narrowed to note the exact time. His heart was pounding with a beat that shocked him because he could not control it. In six minutes, he would see the woman who had filled such a special place in his life for the past thirteen months. He would meet the woman he had never seen, yet whose letters had been with him and had sustained him unfailingly.

He placed himself as close as he could to the information booth. He waited there just beyond the crowd of people besieging the clerks. . . .

Lieutenant Blandford remembered one night in particular, the worst of the fighting, when his plane had been caught in the midst of a pack of enemy fighter planes.

He had seen the grinning face of one of the enemy pilots.

In one of his letters, he had confessed to her that he often felt fear. Just a few days before this battle, he had received her answer.

"Of course you feel fear," she wrote. "All brave men do. Didn't King David know fear? That's why he wrote the twenty-third Psalm. Next time you doubt yourself, I want you to hear my voice reciting to you: 'Yea, though I walk through the valley of the shadow of death, I shall fear no evil, for Thou art with me. . . .'"

And he *had* remembered. He had heard her voice as he imagined it to be, and it had renewed his strength and skill.

Now he was going to hear her real voice. Four minutes to six. He grew tense.

Under the immense roof, people were walking fast, like threads of color being woven into a gray web. A young woman passed close to him and Lieutenant Blandford jumped. She was wearing a red flower in the lapel of her suit. But it was a crimson carnation, not the little red rose they had agreed she would wear to identify her. Besides, this woman was too young, about eighteen years of age, whereas Hollis Meynell had told him that she was thirty.

"Well, what of it?" he had answered. "I'm thirty-two." He was twenty-nine.

His mind went back to that book—the book that had brought them together. It was one of the hundreds of army library books that had been contributed to the Florida training camp. It was called *Of Human Bondage,* and throughout the book were notes in what seemed to be a woman's handwriting. He had always hated that habit of writing things in. But these comments were different. He had never believed that a woman could see into a man's heart so tenderly, so understandingly. Her name was on the bookplate: Hollis Meynell. He had got hold of a New York City telephone book and found her address. He had written, she had answered. Next day he had been shipped out. But they had gone on writing.

For thirteen months, she had faithfully replied—and more than replied. When his letters did not arrive, she wrote anyway. And now he believed he loved her, and she loved him.

But she had refused all his pleas to send him her photograph. That seemed rather bad, of course. But she had explained.

"If your feeling for me is real," she wrote, "what I look like won't matter. Suppose I'm beautiful. I'd always be haunted by the feeling that you had been taking a chance on just that, and that kind of love would be disappointing. Suppose I'm plain (and you must admit that this is more likely). Then I'd always feel that you kept on writing to me only because you were lonely and had no one else. No, don't ask for my picture. When you come to New York, you shall see me. Then you shall make your decision. Remember, each of us is free to stop or to go on after that—whichever we choose. . . ."

One minute to six . . .

Then Lieutenant Blandford's heart leaped higher than his plane had ever done.

A young woman was coming toward him. Her eyes were blue as flowers; her lips and chin had a gentle firmness. In her pale green suit, she was like springtime come alive.

He started toward her, entirely forgetting to notice that she was wearing no rose. Uncontrollably, he took one step closer to her. Then he saw Hollis Meynell.

She was standing almost directly behind the young woman. She was a woman well past forty. Her graying hair was tucked under a worn hat. She was more than plump, and her thick-ankled feet were thrust into low-heeled shoes. But she wore a red rose in the rumpled lapel of her brown coat.

Blandford glanced at the young woman in the green suit who was walking quickly away. His disappointment was keen. Yet deep were his feelings for the woman whose spirit had truly companioned and uplifted his own. And there she stood. Her pale, plump face was gentle and sensible. He could see that now. Her gray eyes had a warm, kindly twinkle.

Lieutenant Blandford did not hesitate. His fingers gripped the small, worn, blue leather copy of *Of Human Bondage* which was to identify him to her. This would not be love, but it would be something precious, something perhaps even rarer than love— a friendship for which he had been and must ever be grateful. . . .

He squared his broad shoulders, saluted, and held the book out toward the woman. While he spoke, he still felt some disappointment.

"I'm Lieutenant John Blandford, and you—you are Miss Meynell. I'm so glad you could meet me. May—may I take you to dinner?"

The woman's face broadened in a pleasant smile. "I don't know what this is all about, son," she answered. "That young lady in the green suit—the one who just went by—begged me to wear this rose on my coat. And she said that if you asked me to go out with you, I should tell you that she's waiting for you in that big restaurant across the street. She said it was some kind of a test. I've got a boy in the army myself, so I didn't mind obliging."

TELLING ABOUT THE STORY. Complete each of the following statements by putting an *x* in the box next to the correct answer. Each statement tells something about the story.

1. Lieutenant Blandford planned to recognize Hollis Meynell
   □ a. because he had a picture of her.
   □ b. because she had sent him a description of herself.
   □ c. by the red rose she had agreed to wear.

2. Hollis Meynell and John Blandford had been brought together
   □ a. by a friend of theirs.
   □ b. through a book.
   □ c. at a party.

3. Hollis's letters to Blandford
   □ a. kept him going through difficult times.
   □ b. were not very important to him.
   □ c. never offered any advice.

4. At the end of the story, we learn that Hollis Meynell
   □ a. was testing Lieutenant Blandford.
   □ b. was more than forty years old.
   □ c. never really cared about Blandford.

□ × 5 = □

NUMBER
CORRECT

YOUR
SCORE

WATCHING FOR NEW VOCABULARY WORDS. Answer the following vocabulary questions by putting an *x* in the box next to the correct response.

1. When Blandford heard Hollis's voice as he imagined it to be, it renewed his strength and skill. The word *renewed* means
   □ a. restored or made fresh again.
   □ b. weakened or reduced in strength.
   □ c. questioned or doubted.

2. For thirteen months, Hollis's letters had sustained Blandford without fail. Which of the following best defines the word *sustained?*
   □ a. hindered
   □ b. supported
   □ c. struggled

3. At first, Blandford thought that the very young woman was Hollis because she wore a crimson flower in the lapel of her suit. What is the meaning of the word *crimson?*
   □ a. broken
   □ b. ugly
   □ c. deep red

4. Blandford waited near the information booth, just beyond the crowd of people besieging the clerks. Define the word *besieging.*
   □ a. admiring
   □ b. helping
   □ c. attacking

□ × 5 = □

NUMBER
CORRECT

YOUR
SCORE

IDENTIFYING STORY ELEMENTS. Each of the following questions tests your understanding of story elements. Put an *x* in the box next to each correct answer.

1. The *setting* of "Appointment with Love" is
   - ☐ a. an army camp.
   - ☐ b. a city street.
   - ☐ c. Grand Central Station.

2. What happened last in the *plot* of the story?
   - ☐ a. Lieutenant Blandford saw a young woman in a pale green suit.
   - ☐ b. Lieutenant Blandford asked the gray-haired woman if she would join him for dinner.
   - ☐ c. Lieutenant Blandford remembered the night when his plane had been caught by enemy fighters.

3. Which statement best *characterizes* John Blandford?
   - ☐ a. He valued beauty more than friendship.
   - ☐ b. He valued friendship more than beauty.
   - ☐ c. He never felt fear.

4. Identify the sentence which best expresses the *theme* of this story.
   - ☐ a. True love passes a test.
   - ☐ b. Absence makes the heart grow fonder.
   - ☐ c. Time flies when you're having fun.

```
┌──────┐        ┌──────┐
│      │ × 5 =  │      │
└──────┘        └──────┘
NUMBER          YOUR
CORRECT         SCORE
```

SELECTING WORDS FROM THE STORY. Complete the following paragraph by filling in each blank with one of the words listed below. Each of the words appears in the story. Since there are five words and four blanks, one word in the group will not be used.

Every day, about half a million people

_____ into Grand Central Station.
         1

In the hustle and bustle of city life, not many

think to look up at the _____
                              2

round clock above the main entrance.

Around the clock, carved out of stone, are

the figures of three Greek gods. Seen

_____ , the clock and the figures
         3

are a powerful sight—a sight that few people

take the _____ to enjoy.
              4

great   fear

crowd

time   together

```
┌──────┐        ┌──────┐
│      │ × 5 =  │      │
└──────┘        └──────┘
NUMBER          YOUR
CORRECT         SCORE
```

THINKING ABOUT THE STORY. Each of the following questions requires you to think critically about the selection. Put an *x* in the box next to the correct answer.

1. We may infer that if Lieutenant Blandford had ignored the gray-haired woman who wore a rose, then Hollis Meynell would
   ☐ a. have been pleased.
   ☐ b. have introduced herself to him.
   ☐ c. not have gone to dinner with him.

2. Probably, Hollis Meynell acted as she did
   ☐ a. because she enjoyed playing amusing games.
   ☐ b. to make fun of Blandford.
   ☐ c. to see what Blandford was really like.

3. Based on his actions in the story, it is fair to say that Lieutenant Blandford
   ☐ a. disappointed Hollis Meynell.
   ☐ b. did not disappoint Hollis Meynell.
   ☐ c. was very foolish.

4. When Lieutenant Blandford and Hollis Meynell meet in the restaurant, he will probably express
   ☐ a. anger.
   ☐ b. delight.
   ☐ c. sorrow.

Thinking More About the Story

- In a letter, Hollis Meynell told Lieutenant Blandford why she did not wish to send him a photograph of herself. Think of at least one additional reason to explain why Hollis was not willing to provide a photograph.
- Do you think that the test that Hollis gave Blandford was a fair one? Was she right to have done this? Give reasons to support your answers.
- Hollis stated that, after they met, she and Blandford would be "free to stop or to go on after that—whichever we choose." Do you think that they decided to continue seeing each other? Explain your answer.

Use the boxes below to total your scores for the exercises.

☐ **T**elling About the Story
+
☐ **W**atching for New Vocabulary Words
+
☐ **I**dentifying Story Elements
+
☐ **S**electing Words from the Story
+
☐ **T**hinking About the Story
▼
☐ **S**core Total: Story 4

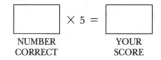

☐ × 5 = ☐

NUMBER   YOUR
CORRECT   SCORE

5. The Journey

by Charles Land

*N*o eighteen-year-old is mature enough to drive across the continent, alone."

Clyde Brenner thought about his father's words. They bothered him. They suggested that Clyde wasn't old enough to take care of himself. Now, Clyde's steady blue eyes followed the highway across the California desert into the rising sun. The new car responded instantly to his touch. It made driving so easy. For a moment, Clyde wished that his father could see him now.

It was at Salome, when he stopped for gas, that Clyde first saw the little red sports car—the Karmann Ghia.

While the attendant pumped the gas, Clyde walked over to the car. The man at the wheel somehow reminded him of his grandfather. He was a man around sixty, cordial, and easy to talk to.

The man grinned. "Want to trade cars?"

"You bet." Clyde said. "I'd do it in a minute if I could."

"Mine is a young person's car," the man went on smiling. "Your new car would suit me better. It's your car, I suppose?"

"Well, it's my dad's," Clyde admitted. "But I'm afraid your car wouldn't suit him either."

"Things are tough all over," laughed the man, as he drove off.

If they are tough at your age, Clyde thought, no wonder they are tough at mine. He had planned this trip with two pals, but at the last minute they had dropped out. So now he was making the trip alone. Clyde was hoping that his dad was not right after all.

While he was thinking about his father, his father was doing something about him. At that very moment, he was in the travel office of Global Oil discussing his problem with Miss Greenwood, the young woman in charge.

"My son has disappeared, and we think you might be able to help us," he was saying. "I understand that about two weeks ago he wrote for maps and a travel route to Massachusetts. His name is Clyde Brenner."

Miss Greenwood found the letter in her files and handed it to Mr. Brenner. His face glowed with pride as he read it.

"Say, this is pretty good. I wonder if I might have it to show to his mother. Clyde is a fine boy, but he doesn't always think things through. We had planned a trip to see his grandmother last winter. But when my business made me change my plans, the disappointment was too much for him. He took off in the family car."

Miss Greenwood was helpful. "Let's look at this map. I can show you the route he's taking. He's driving U.S. 60 to Phoenix and picking up U.S. 66 at Holbrook, Arizona. Then he takes 66 to Chicago and the turnpike to Massachusetts."

"Good," Mr. Brenner said, "then I can alert the police."

Miss Greenwood was shocked.

"Oh, I'm not going to have him picked up. But I do want to talk to him. I don't know if he has enough money to make the trip. We wouldn't have objected if he had someone to go with him. He did have a couple of pals lined up, but you know how kids are—they couldn't raise the cash."

But Clyde didn't know how kids are. He expected his friends to keep their agreement, to raise the money no matter what.

Now, the morning was fresh and clear, the sky a bright blue. The highway reeled out before him as he traveled mile after lonely and desolate mile. He thought of the old days before cars existed, when stage coaches and bandits raced across the sand.

Suddenly, he saw up ahead, on the shoulder of the road, the red Karmann Ghia.

Its friendly owner was waving him down. "Hi, I was hoping you'd come along."

"What happened?" Clyde asked.

"I don't rightly know. She just conked out. Can you give me a lift to the next town?"

"Hop in," Clyde said.

The first thing the man did was reach for the radio dial. "Wonder if we could get some news? I like to keep in touch."

There was no news, but he settled for some music.

"I believe the next town is Aquila," the man said. "I should be able to find a mechanic there."

Clyde assured him that if he couldn't find one in Aquila, then he would take him on to Wickenburg.

"You're a careful driver," said the man after a while. "Never exceed the speed limit do you?"

"I don't want to be picked up," said Clyde.

"Running away?"

"Not exactly."

At that moment the music stopped. A voice said, "We interrupt this program for a special police alert. Authorities are looking for a middle-aged man last seen driving a red Karmann Ghia on Highway 60. If you have any information about this man, call the police immediately. Caution: This man is a killer!"

The man reached over and snapped off the radio. "Now you know," he said. "I don't want to be picked up any more than you do. So let's take it nice and easy. As soon as they find my car, they'll be racing up and down this road like crazy."

Clyde felt himself grow cold all over. "What do you want me to do?" he asked.

The man smiled and took a knife from his pocket. He waved it at Clyde.

"You are going to take me to Phoenix where I can slip out of sight. I could get rid of you and take your driver's license, but luckily for you, I won't be needing a car."

The fear that Clyde had felt was knocked out of him by the shock. His feeling of panic was gone. He drove carefully through Aquila, passing a police car on the way. Clyde made no attempt to alert them. He wondered what his father would do if he were in his place—and eighteen years old.

Then the man nodded toward the rearview window. "There's a car coming fast. It looks like the police."

There was no question about it. With its siren screaming, the prowl car pulled up beside them. The man talked through his teeth. "Sweet talk the cops, or you'll be sorry," he said with emphasis.

The officer leaned out of the window. "Are you Clyde Brenner?"

"Yes, sir."

"Let's see your driver's license."

As one officer checked the license, the other got out of the car and approached them from the other side.

"Who's your passenger?"

"He's no passenger—he's my grandfather."

The officer handed back his driver's license. "Your father is concerned about you. He wants you to call him right away. There's an emergency phone about five miles down the road. You can't miss it. You'll see the box on a telephone pole. I'll follow you and put the call through."

As they drove that last five miles, the man put the knife back into his pocket.

"Good work, kid—that was real nice. Now let me show you how to finish the job. You drive the car right up to the telephone pole. I want to see and hear everything.

I've got a gun in my pocket, so don't try anything smart."

Clyde did as he was told. The man, so close he could reach out and touch the telephone pole, kept his eyes fixed on Clyde.

The officer put through the call. "This is Officer Hathaway of the Arizona State Police. We picked up your son fifteen miles out of Wickenburg. Yes, here he is, Mr. Brenner."

Clyde could hear his father's voice, clear and anxious.

"Are you all right?"

"Yes, Dad, you see I talked Grandfather into going with me."

"You what?"

"Grandfather is here with me. He'll see that everything is okay."

"Listen to me, son. I forgot how mature I was at eighteen. You'll do all right. Now let me talk to the officer."

Clyde handed the phone to the policeman, saying, "Dad wants to thank you."

The officer's eyes narrowed as he heard the voice over the phone. *"Investigate that man!"* said Mr. Brenner. *"The boy's grandfather is dead!"*

41

TELLING ABOUT THE STORY. Complete each of the following statements by putting an *x* in the box next to the correct answer. Each statement tells something about the story.

1. Clyde was upset because his father
   - ☐ a. wouldn't give him money to take a trip.
   - ☐ b. told the police to pick him up.
   - ☐ c. said he wasn't old enough to drive across the country alone.

2. Miss Greenwood was able to tell Mr. Brenner
   - ☐ a. the route that Clyde was taking.
   - ☐ b. that Clyde was in trouble and needed help.
   - ☐ c. where Clyde planned to stay in Massachusetts.

3. The man wanted Clyde to
   - ☐ a. drive him to Chicago to meet a friend.
   - ☐ b. drive him to Phoenix where he planned to slip out of sight.
   - ☐ c. give him his money and the keys to the car.

4. Clyde told the policeman that the man traveling with him was
   - ☐ a. a friend.
   - ☐ b. his grandfather.
   - ☐ c. a killer.

WATCHING FOR NEW VOCABULARY WORDS. Answer the following vocabulary questions by putting an *x* in the box next to the correct response.

1. The man was cordial and easy to talk to. What is the meaning of the word *cordial?*
   - ☐ a. friendly
   - ☐ b. frightened
   - ☐ c. lost

2. Clyde traveled mile after lonely and desolate mile. The word *desolate* means
   - ☐ a. busy.
   - ☐ b. deserted.
   - ☐ c. powerful.

3. The man talked through his teeth and said his words with emphasis. Define the word *emphasis.*
   - ☐ a. great speed
   - ☐ b. lack of concern
   - ☐ c. special force

4. Clyde was careful not to exceed the speed limit because he didn't want to be picked up for speeding. Identify the phrase which best defines the word *exceed.*
   - ☐ a. forget
   - ☐ b. go beyond
   - ☐ c. ask about

☐	× 5 =	☐
NUMBER CORRECT		YOUR SCORE

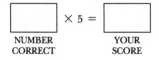

☐	× 5 =	☐
NUMBER CORRECT		YOUR SCORE

IDENTIFYING STORY ELEMENTS. Each of the following questions tests your understanding of story elements. Put an *x* in the box next to each correct answer.

1. The man who Clyde gave a lift to may best be *characterized* as
   ☐ a. pleasant and harmless.
   ☐ b. armed and dangerous.
   ☐ c. young and without money.

2. What happened last in the *plot* of the story?
   ☐ a. Clyde gave a lift to the man who had been driving the sports car.
   ☐ b. Mr. Brenner asked to speak to the officer.
   ☐ c. The policeman asked to see Clyde's driver's license.

3. In "The Journey," there is *conflict* between
   ☐ a. Clyde Brenner and the police.
   ☐ b. Mr. Brenner and Miss Greenwood.
   ☐ c. Clyde and the man he gave a lift to.

4. Which statement best describes the *theme* of this story?
   ☐ a. You can't tell what someone is like by the car he or she drives.
   ☐ b. A young person cannot handle a difficult situation effectively.
   ☐ c. A young man proves he is mature enough to handle a dangerous situation.

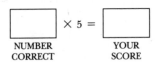

☐	× 5 =	☐
NUMBER CORRECT		YOUR SCORE

SELECTING WORDS FROM THE STORY. Complete the following paragraph by filling in each blank with one of the words listed below. Each of the words appears in the story. Since there are five words and four blanks, one word in the group will not be used.

In the 1840s, hundreds of pioneers headed west to _____ . They usually began their _____ in one of the many towns along the Missouri River. The trail took them across the Great Plains, over the Rocky Mountains, and through the _____ of Utah and Nevada. The trip took many months and was filled with hardships. But acres of rich, fertile land awaited those who were able to _____ the journey.

finish   **trip**

California

passenger   **deserts**

☐	× 5 =	☐
NUMBER CORRECT		YOUR SCORE

43

THINKING ABOUT THE STORY. Each of the following questions requires you to think critically about the selection. Put an *x* in the box next to the correct answer.

1. At the end of the story, Mr. Brenner realized that Clyde was
   □ a. in no danger.
   □ b. sending a signal that something was wrong.
   □ c. eager to return home.

2. We may infer that the police eventually
   □ a. let Clyde and his passenger go.
   □ b. captured the man who was traveling with Clyde.
   □ c. took Clyde back to his father.

3. Evidence at the conclusion of the story suggests that Mr. Brenner
   □ a. was angry at Clyde for leaving with the family car.
   □ b. realized that Clyde was more mature than he had first thought.
   □ c. still thought that Clyde wasn't too mature.

4. One reasonable conclusion to be drawn from this story is that
   □ a. it can be dangerous to pick up a hitchhiker.
   □ b. if you take a long trip, you will probably get into serious trouble.
   □ c. most strangers who act friendly are wanted by the police.

	× 5 =	
NUMBER CORRECT		YOUR SCORE

Thinking More About the Story

● Clyde should have canceled the trip when he learned that his friends could not accompany him. Do you agree or disagree with this statement? Give reasons to support your answer.
● Do you think that Mr. Brenner was right to track down Clyde's travel route and then alert the police to find him? Or should Mr. Brenner have just waited for Clyde to call home? Explain your answer.
● As a result of his experiences in the story, what "lessons" did Clyde learn? Think of at least two. Share them with your classmates.

Use the boxes below to total your scores for the exercises.

	Telling About the Story
+	
	Watching for New Vocabulary Words
+	
	Identifying Story Elements
+	
	Selecting Words from the Story
+	
	Thinking About the Story
▼	
	Score Total: Story 5

44

6. **Thank You, M'am**

by Langston Hughes

*S*he was a large woman with a large purse that had everything in it but hammer and nails. It had a long strap and she carried it slung across her shoulder. It was about eleven o'clock at night, and she was walking alone, when a boy ran up behind her and tried to snatch her purse. The strap broke with the single tug the boy gave it from behind. But the boy's weight, and the weight of the purse combined caused him to lose his balance so, instead of taking off full blast as he had hoped, the boy fell on his back on the sidewalk, and his legs flew up. The large woman simply turned around and kicked him right square in his blue-jeaned sitter. Then she reached down, picked the boy up by his shirt front, and shook him until his teeth rattled.

After that the woman said, "Pick up my pocketbook, and give it here." She still held him. But she bent down enough to permit him to stoop and pick up her purse. Then she said, "Now ain't you ashamed of yourself?"

Firmly gripped by his shirt front, the boy said, "Yes'm."

The woman said, "What did you want to do it for?"

45

The boy said, "I didn't aim to."

She said, "You a lie!"

By that time two or three people passed, stopped, turned to look, and some stood watching.

"If I turn you loose, will you run?" asked the woman.

"Yes'm," said the boy.

"Then I won't turn you loose," said the woman. She did not release him.

"I'm very sorry, lady. I'm sorry," whispered the boy.

"Um-hum! And your face is dirty. I got a great mind to wash your face for you. Ain't you got nobody home to tell you to wash your face?"

"No'm," said the boy.

"Then it will get washed this evening," said the large woman starting up the street, dragging the frightened boy behind her.

He looked as if he were fourteen or fifteen, frail and willow-wild, in tennis shoes and blue jeans.

The woman said, "You ought to be my son. I would teach you right from wrong. Least I can do right now is to wash your face. Are you hungry?"

"No'm," said the being-dragged boy. "I just want you to turn me loose."

"Was I bothering you when I turned that corner?" asked the woman.

"No'm."

"But you put yourself in contact with *me*," said the woman. "If you think that that contact is not going to last awhile, you got another thought coming. When I get through with you, sir, you are going to remember Mrs. Luella Bates Washington Jones."

Sweat popped out on the boy's face and he began to struggle. Mrs. Jones stopped, jerked him around in front of her, put a half nelson about his neck, and continued to drag him up the street. When she got to her door, she dragged the boy inside, down a hall, and into a large kitchenette-furnished room at the rear of the house. She switched on the light and left the door open. The boy could hear other roomers laughing and talking in the large house. Some of their doors were open, too, so he knew he and the woman were not alone. The woman still had him by the neck in the middle of her room.

She said, "What is your name?"

"Roger," answered the boy.

"Then, Roger, you go to that sink and wash your face," said the woman, whereupon she turned him loose—at last. Roger looked at the door—looked at the woman—looked at the door—*and went to the sink.*

"Let the water run until it gets warm," she said. "Here's a clean towel."

"You gonna take me to jail?" asked the boy, bending over the sink.

"Not with that face, I would not take you nowhere," said the woman. "Here I am trying to get home to cook me a bite to eat and you snatch my pocketbook! Maybe you ain't been to your supper either, late as it be. Have you?"

"There's nobody home at my house," said the boy.

"Then we'll eat," said the woman. "I believe you're hungry—or been hungry—to try to snatch my pocketbook."

"I wanted a pair of blue suede shoes," said the boy.

"Well, you didn't have to snatch my pocketbook to get some suede shoes," said

Mrs. Luella Bates Washington Jones. "You could of asked me."

"M'am?"

The water dripping from his face, the boy looked at her. There was a long pause. A very long pause. After he had dried his face and not knowing what else to do dried it again, the boy turned around, wondering what next. The door was open. He could make a dash for it down the hall. He could run, run, run, run, *run!*

The woman was sitting on the daybed. After a while she said, "I were young once and I wanted things I could not get."

There was another long pause. The boy's mouth opened. Then he frowned, but not knowing he frowned.

The woman said, "Um-hum! You thought I was going to say *but,* didn't you? You thought I was going to say, *but I didn't snatch people's pocketbooks.* Well, I wasn't going to say that." Pause. Silence. "I have done things, too, which I would not tell you, son—neither tell God, if He didn't already know. So you set down while I fix us something to eat. You might run that comb through your hair so you will look presentable."

In another corner of the room behind a screen was a gas plate and an icebox. Mrs. Jones got up and went behind the screen. The woman did not watch the boy to see if he was going to run now, nor did she watch her purse which she left behind her on the daybed. But the boy took care to sit on the far side of the room where he thought she could easily see him out of the corner of her eye, if she wanted to. He did not trust the woman *not* to trust him. And he did not want to be mistrusted now.

"Do you need somebody to go to the store?" asked the boy, "Maybe to get some milk or something?"

"Don't believe I do," said the woman, "unless you just want sweet milk yourself. I was going to make cocoa out of this canned milk I got here."

"That will be fine," said the boy.

She heated some lima beans and ham she had in the icebox, made the cocoa, and set the table. The woman did not ask the boy anything about where he lived, or his folks, or anything else that would embarrass him. Instead, as they ate, she told him about her job in a hotel beauty shop that stayed open late, what the work was like, and how all kinds of women came in and out, blonds, redheads, and brunettes. Then she cut him a half of her ten-cent cake.

"Eat some more, son," she said.

When they were finished eating, she got up and said, "Now, here, take this ten dollars and buy yourself some blue suede shoes. And next time, do not make the mistake of latching onto *my* pocketbook *nor nobody else's*—because shoes come by devilish ways like that will burn your feet. I got to get my rest now. But I wish you would behave yourself, son, from here on in."

She led him down the hall to the front door and opened it. "Goodnight! Behave yourself!" she said, looking out into the street.

The boy wanted to say something else other than, "Thank you, m'am," to Mrs. Luella Bates Washington Jones, but he couldn't do so as he turned at the barren stoop and looked back at the large woman in the door. He barely managed to say, "Thank you," before she shut the door. And he never saw her again.

TELLING ABOUT THE STORY. Complete each of the following statements by putting an *x* in the box next to the correct answer. Each statement tells something about the story.

1. When Roger attempted to steal Mrs. Jones's purse, he
   ☐ a. shouted at her to frighten her.
   ☐ b. grabbed it and began to run.
   ☐ c. lost his balance and fell.

2. Mrs. Jones said that if Roger were her son, she would
   ☐ a. punish him severely.
   ☐ b. teach him right from wrong.
   ☐ c. report him to the police.

3. Roger wanted to steal the pocketbook to
   ☐ a. buy food.
   ☐ b. buy some blue jeans.
   ☐ c. get some suede shoes.

4. At the end of the story, Mrs. Jones advised Roger to
   ☐ a. help others.
   ☐ b. behave himself.
   ☐ c. get a good education.

WATCHING FOR NEW VOCABULARY WORDS. Answer the following vocabulary questions by putting an *x* in the box next to the correct response.

1. Mrs. Jones suggested that Roger comb his hair to make himself presentable. The word *presentable* means
   ☐ a. suitable or fit to be seen.
   ☐ b. worthy of receiving a present or gift.
   ☐ c. older looking or more mature.

2. Roger sat where Mrs. Jones could easily see him because he didn't want to be mistrusted by her. Define the word *mistrusted.*
   ☐ a. struck or hit
   ☐ b. doubted or not believed
   ☐ c. shouted at or screamed at

3. Mrs. Jones stated that blonds, redheads, and brunettes came to the beauty shop where she worked. *Brunettes* have
   ☐ a. red hair.
   ☐ b. blond hair.
   ☐ c. dark brown or black hair.

4. Roger made a mistake by latching onto Mrs. Jones's pocketbook. As used in this sentence, what is the meaning of the word *latching?*
   ☐ a. seizing hold of
   ☐ b. locking with a bar
   ☐ c. cutting with a sharp instrument

	× 5 =	
NUMBER CORRECT		YOUR SCORE

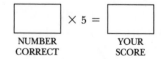

	× 5 =	
NUMBER CORRECT		YOUR SCORE

IDENTIFYING STORY ELEMENTS. Each of the following questions tests your understanding of story elements. Put an *x* in the box next to each correct answer.

1. "Thank you, M'am" is *set*
   ☐ a. early one morning.
   ☐ b. in the afternoon.
   ☐ c. late one evening.

2. What happened last in the *plot* of the story?
   ☐ a. Roger thanked Mrs. Jones.
   ☐ b. Mrs. Jones shook Roger until his teeth rattled.
   ☐ c. Roger offered to go to the store to buy milk.

3. Which statement best *characterizes* Mrs. Luella Bates Washington Jones?
   ☐ a. Because she was wealthy, she was willing to share things with others.
   ☐ b. She was kind, generous, loving, and understanding.
   ☐ c. Her experiences had taught her not to trust anyone.

4. What is the *mood* of "Thank you, M'am"?
   ☐ a. tragic
   ☐ b. comic
   ☐ c. mysterious

SELECTING WORDS FROM THE STORY. Complete the following paragraph by filling in each blank with one of the words listed below. Each of the words appears in the story. Since there are five words and four blanks, one word in the group will not be used.

Langston Hughes is _____ for

his many poems and stories about the black

experience. For a number of years, Hughes

_____ in Harlem in New York City.

As he walked its streets, shopped in its stores,

and took part in its activities, he made

_____ with the people he would

eventually write about. During a writing

career that _____ forty years,

Hughes published more than fifty books.

lived   purse

contact

remembered   lasted

| | ☐ × 5 = | ☐ |
| NUMBER CORRECT | | YOUR SCORE |

| | ☐ × 5 = | ☐ |
| NUMBER CORRECT | | YOUR SCORE |

49

THINKING ABOUT THE STORY. Each of the following questions requires you to think critically about the selection. Put an *x* in the box next to the correct answer.

1. Clues in the story suggest that Mrs. Jones took Roger to a
   - ☐ a. fancy apartment house.
   - ☐ b. hotel.
   - ☐ c. rooming house.

2. Probably, Mrs. Jones gained Roger's confidence when she
   - ☐ a. confided that she, too, had done things which embarrassed her.
   - ☐ b. called Roger a liar.
   - ☐ c. asked Roger if he wasn't ashamed of himself.

3. Mrs. Jones said that shoes come by devilish ways will burn your feet. Which of the following best expresses the meaning of this sentence?
   - ☐ a. It is most economical to buy shoes of high quality.
   - ☐ b. It is not possible to profit from gains achieved through evil means.
   - ☐ c. One should always treat people with respect.

4. It is fair to say that Mrs. Jones
   - ☐ a. was afraid of Roger.
   - ☐ b. expected Roger to pay back the money she gave him.
   - ☐ c. taught Roger a valuable lesson.

	× 5 =	
NUMBER CORRECT		YOUR SCORE

Thinking More About the Story

- Mrs. Jones told Roger, "When I get through with you, sir, you are going to remember Mrs. Luella Bates Washington Jones." We know that Roger never saw Mrs. Jones again. Did he ever forget her? Explain your answer.
- At first, Roger attempted to steal Mrs. Jones's purse. Later, she left the purse on the bed and did not even watch it. Why wasn't Mrs. Jones worried about leaving her purse on the bed? Why didn't Roger try to steal it?
- Mrs. Jones may be described as a person of high principles. Find examples from the story to support this statement.

Use the boxes below to total your scores for the exercises.

☐ +	**T**elling About the Story
☐ +	**W**atching for New Vocabulary Words
☐ +	**I**dentifying Story Elements
☐ +	**S**electing Words from the Story
☐ ▼	**T**hinking About the Story
☐	**S**core Total: Story 6

7. Sarah Tops

by Isaac Asimov

I came out of the Museum of Natural History and was crossing the street on my way to the subway, when I saw the crowd about halfway down the block; and the police cars, too. I could hear the whine of an ambulance.

For a minute, I hesitated, but then I walked on. The crowds of the curious just get in the way of officials trying to save lives. Dad, who's a detective on the force, complains about that all the time.

I just kept my mind on the term paper I was going to have to write on air pollution for my eighth-grade class, and mentally arranged the notes I had taken during the museum program on the subject.

Of course, I knew I would read about it in the afternoon papers. Besides, I would ask Dad about it after dinner. He sometimes talked about cases without telling too much of the real security details.

51

After I asked, Mom looked kind of funny and said, "The man was in the museum when he was killed."

I said, "I was working on my term paper. I was there first thing in the morning."

Mom looked very worried. "There might have been shooting in the museum."

"Well, there wasn't," said Dad, soothingly. "This man tried to lose himself there and he didn't succeed."

"*I* would have," I said. "I know the museum, every inch."

Dad doesn't like me bragging, so he frowned a little and said, "They didn't let him get away entirely—caught up with him outside, knifed him, and got away. We'll catch them, though. We know who they are."

He nodded his head. "They're what's left of the gang that broke into that jewelry store two weeks ago. We managed to get the jewels back, but we didn't grab all the men. And not all the jewels either. One diamond was left. A big one—worth $30,000."

"Maybe that's what the killers were after," I said.

"Very likely. The dead man was probably trying to cross the other two and get away with that one stone for himself. They turned out his pockets, practically ripped off his clothes, after they knifed him."

"Did they get the diamond?" I asked.

"How can we tell? The woman who reported the killing came on him when he was still just barely alive. She said he said three words to her, very slowly, 'Try—Sarah—Tops.' Then he died."

"Who is Sarah Tops?" asked Mom.

Dad shrugged. "I don't know. I don't even know if that's really what he said. The woman was pretty hysterical. If she's right and that's what he said then maybe the killers didn't get the diamond. Maybe the dead man left it with Sarah Tops, whoever she is. Maybe he knew he was dying and wanted to have it off his conscience."

"Is there a Sarah Tops in the phone book, Dad?" I asked.

Dad said, "Did you think we didn't look? No Sarah Tops, either one *P* or two *P*s. Nothing in the city directory. Nothing in our files. Nothing in the FBI files."

Mom said, "Maybe it's not a person. Maybe it's a firm. Sarah Tops Cakes or something."

"Could be," said Dad. "There's no Sarah Tops firm, but there are other types of Tops companies and they'll be checked for anyone working there named Sarah."

I got an idea suddenly and bubbled over. "Listen, Dad, maybe it isn't a firm either. Maybe it's a *thing*. Maybe the woman didn't hear 'Sarah Tops' but 'Sarah's top'; you know, a *top* that you spin. If the dead guy has a daughter named Sarah, maybe he gouged a bit out of her top and stashed the diamond inside and——"

Dad grinned. "Very good, Larry," he said. "But he doesn't have a daughter named Sarah. Or any relative by that name as far as we know. We've searched where he lived and there's nothing reported there that can be called a top."

"Well," I said, sort of let down and disappointed, "I suppose that's not such a good idea anyway, because why should he say we ought to *try* it? He either hid it in Sarah's top or he didn't. He would know which. Why should he say we should *try* it?"

And then it hit me. What if——

I said, "Dad, can you get into the museum this late?"

"On police business? Sure."

"Dad," I said, kind of breathless, "I think we better go look. *Now.* Before the people start coming in again."

"Why?"

"I've got a silly idea. I—I——"

Dad didn't push me. He likes me to have my own ideas. He thinks maybe I'll be a detective too, some day. He said, "All right. Let's follow up your lead."

We got there just when the last purple bit of twilight was turning to black. We were let in by a guard.

I'd never been in the museum when it was dark. It looked like a huge, underground cave, with the guard's flashlight seeming to make things even more mysterious.

We took the elevator up to the fourth floor, where the big shapes loomed in the bit of light that shone this way and that as the guard moved his flash. "Do you want me to put on the light in this room?" he asked.

"Yes, please," I said.

There they all were. Some in glass cases; but the big ones in the middle of the large room. Bones and teeth and spines of giants that ruled the earth, millions of years ago. I said, "I want to look close at that one. Is it all right if I climb over the railing?"

"Go ahead," said the guard. He helped me.

I leaned against the platform, looking at the grayish plaster material the skeleton was standing on.

"What's this?" I said. It didn't look much different in color from the plaster.

"Chewing gum," said the guard, frowning. "Those darn kids——"

I said, "The guy was trying to get away and he saw his chance to throw this—hide it from the gang——"

Dad took the gum from me, squeezed it, and then pulled it apart. Inside, something caught the light and *flashed.* Dad put it in an envelope and said to me, "How did you know?"

I said, "Well, look at it."

It was a magnificent skeleton. It had a large skull with bone stretching back over the neck vertebrae. It had two horns over the eyes, and a third one, just a bump, on the snout. The nameplate said: *Triceratops.*

TELLING ABOUT THE STORY. Complete each of the following statements by putting an *x* in the box next to the correct answer. Each statement tells something about the story.

1. According to Dad, the man went into the museum because he
   - ☐ a. had arranged to meet his daughter there.
   - ☐ b. was interested in giant creatures that lived millions of years ago.
   - ☐ c. was trying to hide there.

2. The killers appeared to be searching for
   - ☐ a. a large diamond.
   - ☐ b. a bag of jewels.
   - ☐ c. thirty-thousand dollars in cash.

3. Larry asked his father if it was possible to
   - ☐ a. question everyone named Sarah Tops.
   - ☐ b. get into the museum that late.
   - ☐ c. request help from the FBI.

4. The dying man's last words indicated
   - ☐ a. who the murderers were.
   - ☐ b. that he was sorry for what he had done.
   - ☐ c. where the diamond could be found.

WATCHING FOR NEW VOCABULARY WORDS. Answer the following vocabulary questions by putting an *x* in the box next to the correct response.

1. As Larry thought about the term paper he had to write, he mentally arranged the notes he had taken. *Mentally* refers to
   - ☐ a. strength and power.
   - ☐ b. the mind.
   - ☐ c. swiftness or speed.

2. Dad said it was possible that the dying man left the stolen diamond with someone named Sarah Tops in order to have the theft off his conscience. Which expression best defines the word *conscience?*
   - ☐ a. a sense of right and wrong
   - ☐ b. a burst of energy
   - ☐ c. a loss of control

3. It was a magnificent skeleton with a large skull. What is the meaning of the word *magnificent?*
   - ☐ a. little or small
   - ☐ b. splendid or grand
   - ☐ c. very disappointing

4. Larry wondered if the man had gouged a bit out of a wooden top and hidden the diamond there. As used here, the word *gouged* means
   - ☐ a. tricked.
   - ☐ b. decorated.
   - ☐ c. dug out.

	× 5 =	
NUMBER CORRECT		YOUR SCORE

	× 5 =	
NUMBER CORRECT		YOUR SCORE

54

IDENTIFYING STORY ELEMENTS. Each of the following questions tests your understanding of story elements. Put an *x* in the box next to each correct answer.

1. The *main character* of this story is
   ☐ a. Larry.
   ☐ b. Dad.
   ☐ c. Mom.

2. What happened first in the *plot* of the story?
   ☐ a. The guard let Larry and his father into the museum.
   ☐ b. Larry saw a crowd of people and police cars.
   ☐ c. Mom suggested that Sarah Tops might be the name of a firm rather than a person.

3. Where is "Sarah Tops" *set?*
   ☐ a. in a small village
   ☐ b. in a quiet town
   ☐ c. in a large city

4. Select the statement that best expresses the *theme* of this story.
   ☐ a. A detective's son solves a puzzling case.
   ☐ b. Two thieves murder a man who tried to double-cross them.
   ☐ c. The police break up a gang and recover some jewels.

	× 5 =	
NUMBER CORRECT		YOUR SCORE

SELECTING WORDS FROM THE STORY. Complete the following paragraph by filling in each blank with one of the words listed below. Each of the words appears in the story. Since there are five words and four blanks, one word in the group will not be used.

When you think about dinosaurs, you

_____ imagine huge animals that
          1

weigh many tons. Some dinosaurs were

indeed _____—almost 90 feet
              2

long and 20 feet high. But you may

be surprised to learn that dinosaur

_____ reveal that some dinosaurs
          3

were rather small. One kind was about

2½ feet long. But large or small, these

creatures, which once ruled the

_____, all had very tiny brains.
          4

giants   museum

earth

bones   probably

	× 5 =	
NUMBER CORRECT		YOUR SCORE

55

THINKING ABOUT THE STORY. Each of the following questions requires you to think critically about the selection. Put an *x* in the box next to the correct answer.

1. Larry wanted to go to the museum right away because he
   - [ ] a. enjoyed visiting the museum when it wasn't too crowded.
   - [ ] b. was too busy to go to the museum the following day.
   - [ ] c. was afraid that someone would find the diamond before he did.

2. Clues in the story indicate that the dying man hid the diamond
   - [ ] a. in a wooden top.
   - [ ] b. in some chewing gum.
   - [ ] c. somewhere in his clothing.

3. Which statement is true?
   - [ ] a. The police interviewed several people named Sarah Tops.
   - [ ] b. The murderers had almost found the diamond.
   - [ ] c. The dying man was trying to say "triceratops."

4. You can conclude that the man
   - [ ] a. planned to sell the diamond and give the money to charity.
   - [ ] b. was going to return to the museum later to get the diamond.
   - [ ] c. wanted to tell the gang where the diamond could be found.

	× 5 =	
NUMBER CORRECT		YOUR SCORE

Thinking More About the Story

- Dad thought that Larry might be a detective one day. Do you believe that Larry would make a good detective? Present evidence from the story to support your opinion.
- Suppose that Larry hadn't found the diamond. What do you think would have happened to it? Give two different, but likely, answers.
- It is obvious why this story is called "Sarah Tops." Think of another title that is also appropriate. Explain your choice.

Use the boxes below to total your scores for the exercises.

	Telling About the Story
+	
	Watching for New Vocabulary Words
+	
	Identifying Story Elements
+	
	Selecting Words from the Story
+	
	Thinking About the Story
▼	
	Score Total: Story 7

8. Louisa, Please Come Home

by Shirley Jackson

I listened to my mother's voice over the radio. "Louisa," she said, "please come home. It's been three years since we saw you. We all miss you. We want you back again. Louisa, please come home."

Once a year I heard that, on the anniversary of the day I ran away. I also read the newspaper stories. "Louisa Tether vanished one year ago." Or two years, or three. I used to wait for June 20 as if it were my birthday.

I was living in Chandler, which was a big enough city for me to hide in. It was also near my old home, so the papers always made a big fuss about my anniversary.

I didn't decide to leave on the spur of the moment. I had been planning it for a long time. Everything had to go right. If it had gone wrong, I would have looked like an awful fool, and my sister Carol would never have let me forget that.

I planned it for the day before her wedding. The papers said they had the wedding anyway. Carol told a reporter that her sister Louisa would have wanted it that way.

"She would never have wanted to spoil my wedding," Carol said, knowing that was exactly what I'd wanted.

Anyway, everyone was hurrying around the house, getting ready for the wedding. I just walked out the door and started off.

There was only one bad minute, when Paul saw me. Paul has always lived next door to us, and Carol hates him more than she hates me. My mother can't stand him, either.

Of course, he didn't know I was running away. I told him what I had told my parents. I was going downtown to get away from all the confusion. He wanted to come with me, but I ran for the bus and left him standing there.

I took the bus downtown and walked to the railroad station. I bought a round-trip ticket. That would make them think I was coming back. Then they wouldn't start looking for me too quickly.

I knew they'd think I'd stay in Crain, which was the biggest city the train went to. So I stayed there only one day.

I bought a tan raincoat in a department store in Crain. I had left home wearing a new jacket. I just left it on a counter in the store. Someone probably bought it.

I was pretty sure of one thing. There must be thousands of 19-year-old girls, fair-haired, five feet four inches tall, weighing 126 pounds, and a lot of them would be wearing tan raincoats.

It's funny how no one pays any attention to you. Hundreds of people saw me that day, but no one really *saw* me.

I took a train to Chandler, where I had been heading all along. I slept on the train.

When I got to Chandler, I bought a suitcase, some stockings, and a little clock. I put everything in the suitcase. Then I was ready to get myself settled in Chandler. Nothing is hard to do unless you get upset or excited about it.

I decided who I was going to be. I was a 19-year-old girl named Lois Taylor, who had a nice family upstate. I had saved enough money to come to live in Chandler. When the summer was over, I would go to the business school there. I would need a job to pay for the school.

I stopped in a drugstore for breakfast and a paper. I read the ads for furnished rooms. It all looked so normal. Suitcase, raincoat, rooms for rent. When I asked the clerk how to get to Primrose Street, he never even looked at me.

I walked into Mrs. Peacock's house on Primrose Street. I knew this was the perfect place. My room was nice, and Mrs. Peacock and I liked each other.

She was pleased that my mother wanted me to find a clean room in a good neighborhood, and that I wanted to save money so I could send some home every week.

Within an hour, Mrs. Peacock knew all about my imaginary family. I told her my mother was a widow. My sister had just been married, and my younger brother Paul made my mother worry a lot. He didn't want to settle down.

Mrs. Peacock wanted to take care of me. She told me about a job in a neighborhood stationery store. So there I was. I had been away from home for 24 hours, and I was a whole new person. I was Lois Taylor, who lived on Primrose Street and worked at the stationery store.

Mrs. Peacock and I would read the papers during breakfast. She'd ask my opinion about the girl who disappeared over in Rockville. I'd say she must be crazy to leave a nice home like that.

Once I picked up the paper and looked at the picture. "Do you think she looks like me?" I asked Mrs. Peacock.

Mrs. Peacock said, "No. Her hair is longer, and her face is fatter."

"I think she looks like me," I said.

My picture was in the Chandler papers a lot, but no one ever looked at me twice. I went to work. I shopped in the stores. I went to the movies and the beach with Mrs. Peacock, and no one recognized me. I had done a perfect job of changing my identity.

One morning, Mrs. Peacock was reading about my disappearance. "They're saying now that she was kidnapped," she said.

"I feel kind of sorry for her," I said.

"You can't ever tell," she said. "Maybe she went willingly with the kidnapper."

On the anniversary of my running away, I treated myself to a new hat. When I got home, Mrs. Peacock was listening to the radio, and I heard my mother's voice.

"Louisa," she said, "please come home."

"That poor woman," Mrs. Peacock said. "Imagine how she must feel. She hasn't given up hope of finding her little girl alive some day."

I had decided not to go to business school, because the stationery store was branching

out. I would probably be a manager soon. Mrs. Peacock and I agreed it would be foolish to give up such a good job.

By this time, I had some money in the bank, and I was getting along fine. I never had a thought about going back. It was just plain bad luck that I had to meet Paul.

I didn't stop to think when I saw him on the street. I yelled, "Paul!"

He turned around and stared at me. Then he said, "Is it possible?"

He said I had to go back. If I didn't, he'd tell them where I was. He told me there was still a reward for anyone who found me. He said I could run away again after he collected the reward.

Maybe I really wanted to go home, and that's why I yelled his name out on the street. Anyway, I decided to go with him.

I told Mrs. Peacock I was going to visit my family upstate. I thought that was funny. Paul sent a telegram to my parents.

When we got to Rockville, we took a taxi. I began to get nervous, looking out the window. I would have sworn that I hadn't thought about Rockville for three years, but I remembered it all, as if I had never been away.

The taxi turned into my street. When I saw the house, I almost cried. "Everything looks just the same," I said. "I caught the bus right there on the corner."

"If I had managed to stop you," Paul said, "you probably wouldn't have tried again."

We walked up the driveway. I wondered if they were watching from the window, and if I would have to ring the doorbell. I had never had to ring it before.

I was still wondering when Carol opened the door. "Carol!" I said. I was honestly glad to see her.

She looked at me hard. Then she stepped back, and I saw my mother and father. I was going to run to them, but I held myself back. I wasn't sure if they were angry with me or happy that I was back.

I wasn't sure of what to say, so I just stood there and said, "Mother?"

She put her hands on my shoulders and looked at my face for a long time. She was crying, and she looked old and sad. Then she turned to Paul and said, "How could you do this to me again?"

Paul was frightened. "Mrs. Tether—"

My mother asked me, "What is your name, dear?"

"Louisa Tether," I said stupidly.

"No, dear," she said very gently. "Your *real* name."

"Now I felt like crying. "Louisa Tether," I said. "That's my name."

"Why don't you people leave us alone?" Carol screamed. "We've spent years trying to find my sister, and people like you just try to cheat us out of the reward money."

"Carol," my father said, "you're frightening the poor child. Young lady," he said to me, "I don't think you realized how cruel this would be to us. You look like a nice girl. Try to imagine your own mother if someone did this to her."

I tried to imagine my own mother. I looked straight at her.

My father said, "I'm sure this young man didn't tell you he's done this twice before. He's brought us girls who pretended to be our Louisa. The first time we were fooled for several days. The girl *looked* like our Louisa and *acted* like our Louisa. She even

knew about family things that only Louisa—or Paul—could know. But she was not our daughter, and my wife suffers more each time her hopes are raised."

He put one arm around my mother and the other around Carol. They all stood there looking at me.

Paul started to argue with them. I realized that all I wanted was to stay here, but I couldn't. They had made up their minds that I wasn't Louisa.

"Paul," I said, "can't you see that you're only making Mr. Tether angry?"

"Correct, young lady," my father said.

"Paul," I said, "these people don't want us here." Paul was about to argue again. Instead, he turned and walked out.

I turned to follow him. My father—I mean Mr. Tether—took my hand. "My daughter was younger than you," he said gently. "But I'm sure you have a family somewhere. Go back to the people who love you."

That meant Mrs. Peacock, I guess.

"To make sure you get there," my father said, "I want you to take this." He put a $20 bill in my hand. "I hope someone will do as much for our Louisa."

"Good-bye, my dear," my mother said. "Good luck to you."

"I hope your daughter comes back some day," I told them. "Good-bye."

I gave the money to Paul. He'd gone to a lot of trouble, and I still had my job at the stationery store.

My mother still talks to me on the radio once a year. "Louisa," she says, "please come home. We miss you so much. Your mother and father love you and will never forget you. Louisa, please come home."

TELLING ABOUT THE STORY. Complete each of the following statements by putting an *x* in the box next to the correct answer. Each statement tells something about the story.

1. Louisa Tether left home
   - ☐ a. exactly one year ago.
   - ☐ b. three years ago.
   - ☐ c. about ten years ago.

2. Louisa told Mrs. Peacock
   - ☐ a. all about her sister, Carol.
   - ☐ b. about her imaginary family.
   - ☐ c. that she had run away from home.

3. At Chandler, Paul told Louisa that
   - ☐ a. her family had forgotten all about her.
   - ☐ b. many other young women had pretended to be her.
   - ☐ c. there was still a reward for anyone who found her.

4. When Louisa returned home to her family, they
   - ☐ a. greeted her warmly.
   - ☐ b. didn't recognize her.
   - ☐ c. scolded her for running away.

WATCHING FOR NEW VOCABULARY WORDS. Answer the following vocabulary questions by putting an *x* in the box next to the correct response.

1. As everyone bustled about, Louisa said that she was going downtown to get away from all the confusion. Which of the following best defines the word *confusion?*
   - ☐ a. lack of order
   - ☐ b. pain or hurt
   - ☐ c. friends and relatives

2. Louisa didn't decide to leave on the spur of the moment; she had been planning it for a long time. The expression *on the spur of the moment* means
   - ☐ a. with a goal in mind.
   - ☐ b. without a good reason.
   - ☐ c. on a sudden impulse.

3. In Chandler, Louisa looked in the newspaper at ads for furnished rooms. The word *furnished* means
   - ☐ a. old and run-down.
   - ☐ b. equipped with furniture.
   - ☐ c. very expensive.

4. No one recognized Louisa because she had done a perfect job of changing her identity. Select the answer which best defines the word *identity.*
   - ☐ a. characteristics
   - ☐ b. job
   - ☐ c. address

	× 5 =	
NUMBER CORRECT		YOUR SCORE

	× 5 =	
NUMBER CORRECT		YOUR SCORE

61

IDENTIFYING STORY ELEMENTS. Each of the following questions tests your understanding of story elements. Put an *x* in the box next to each correct answer.

1. The *main character* in this story is
   ☐ a. Louisa.
   ☐ b. Paul.
   ☐ c. Mrs. Peacock.

2. What happened first in the *plot* of "Louisa, Please Come Home"?
   ☐ a. Louisa went to Chandler where she bought a suitcase and a clock.
   ☐ b. Louisa's mother asked her what her *real* name was.
   ☐ c. Mr. Tether gave Louisa twenty dollars.

3. This story is *set* in
   ☐ a. a stationery store.
   ☐ b. a bus and a train.
   ☐ c. two cities not very far from each other.

4. The *mood* of "Louisa, Please Come Home" may best be described as
   ☐ a. bright and cheerful.
   ☐ b. comic and amusing.
   ☐ c. sad and distressing.

SELECTING WORDS FROM THE STORY. Complete the following paragraph by filling in each blank with one of the words listed below. Each of the words appears in the story. Since there are five words and four blanks, one word in the group will not be used.

Before television was invented, people eagerly _____ to the radio. Families laughed at _____ performers such as Bob Hope, Jack Benny, and George Burns and Gracie Allen. The voices of news broadcasters Lowell Thomas and Edward R. Murrow were _____ by millions. Singers such as Kate Smith and Bing Crosby became famous. You can still hear radio shows today, but most people would agree that the golden age of radio is now _____ .

recognized   telegram

over

listened   funny

NUMBER CORRECT	× 5 =	YOUR SCORE

NUMBER CORRECT	× 5 =	YOUR SCORE

THINKING ABOUT THE STORY. Each of the following questions requires you to think critically about the selection. Put an *x* in the box next to the correct answer.

1. Evidence in the story suggests that
   □ a. Louisa and her sister didn't get along well with each other.
   □ b. Mr. and Mrs. Tether will eventually find their lost daughter.
   □ c. Louisa will return home again.

2. We may infer that Louisa was hoping that her family would
   □ a. send her some money.
   □ b. welcome her back.
   □ c. move to Chandler to be near her.

3. Which one of the following statements is true?
   □ a. Mrs. Peacock knew that Lois Taylor was actually Louisa Tether.
   □ b. At the end of the story, Louisa realized that it was pointless to try to change her parents' minds.
   □ c. When Louisa returned to Rockville, she felt comfortable and at ease.

4. Louisa stated, "My father—I mean Mr. Tether—took my hand." This suggests that Louisa
   □ a. was too confused to think clearly.
   □ b. was pleased with her father's actions.
   □ c. felt that she no longer really had a father.

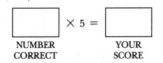

	× 5 =	
NUMBER CORRECT		YOUR SCORE

Thinking More About the Story

- When Louisa returned home, Mr. Tether told her, "My daughter was younger than you." Perhaps Louisa looked older now because she had left home years before. What other reasons might explain why Louisa's family didn't recognize her?
- Louisa said that "Nothing is hard to do unless you get upset or excited about it." Show how Louisa's actions illustrate this statement. What do these words suggest about how Louisa will manage in the future?
- If Louisa had the opportunity to "do it all over," would she run away from home again? Explain.

Use the boxes below to total your scores for the exercises.

	Telling About the Story
+	
	Watching for New Vocabulary Words
+	
	Identifying Story Elements
+	
	Selecting Words from the Story
+	
	Thinking About the Story
▼	
	Score Total: Story 8

9. A Dip in the Poole

by Bill Pronzini

I was sitting in a large comfortable leather armchair in the lobby of the Hotel Poole, leafing through a magazine, when the young woman in the dark tweed suit picked Andrew J. Stuyvesant's pocket.

She did it very cleverly. Stuyvesant—a silver-haired old gentleman who carries a walking stick and is worth fifteen or twenty million dollars—had just stepped out of one of the elevators in front of me.

The young woman appeared from the direction of the marble staircase. Walking rapidly, and pretending to be absorbed in thought, she bumped into him. She then appeared embarrassed and apologized. Stuyvesant bowed in a gallant way, saying, "Why that's perfectly all right."

I could see that she got his wallet and the diamond stickpin from his tie. Stuyvesant neither felt nor suspected a thing.

The young woman apologized again and then hurried off across the thick carpeting toward the main entrance at the end of the room. As she moved, she skillfully slipped the items into a tan suede bag she carried over one arm.

Immediately, I popped out of my chair and moved quickly after her. She managed to get within a few steps of the glass doors before I caught up with her.

I let my hand fall on her arm. "Excuse me just a moment," I said, smiling.

She stiffened, becoming completely still. Then she turned and regarded me icily. "I beg your pardon," she said in a frosty voice.

"You and I had best have a little chat."

"I am not in the habit of chatting with men I don't know."

"I think you'll make an exception in my case," I said.

Her brown eyes flashed angrily as she said, "I suggest you let go of my arm. If you don't, I shall call the manager."

I shrugged lightly. "There's no need for that."

"I certainly hope not."

"Simply because he would only call for me."

"What?"

"I'm the chief of security at the Hotel Poole, you see," I told her. "I'm what once was referred to as the house detective."

She grew pale, and the light dimmed in her eyes. "Oh," she said softly.

At my direction, we moved toward the hotel's lounge, a short distance on our left. She sat down in one of the leather booths and I seated myself opposite. A waiter approached, but I shook my head and he retreated.

I looked at the young woman on the other side of the table. The soft glow from the candle in its center gave her classic features the impression of purity and innocence.

"Without a doubt," I said, "you're the most beautiful dip I've ever encountered."

"I . . . don't know what you're talking about," she said.

"Don't you?"

"Certainly not."

"A *dip* is underworld slang for a pickpocket."

She pretended to be insulted. "Are you suggesting that I . . . ?"

"Oh, come now," I said. "There's no purpose to be served in continuing this act. I saw you lift Mr. Stuyvesant's wallet and his diamond stickpin. I was sitting directly across from the elevator, not fifteen feet away."

She didn't say anything. Her fingers drummed over her tan suede bag. After a moment, her eyes lifted to mine, briefly, and then dropped to the bag again. She sighed in a tortured way. "You're right, of course," she finally said. "I stole those things."

I reached out, gently took the bag from her and snapped it open. Stuyvesant's wallet and stickpin rested on top of the various articles inside. I removed them, reclosed the bag and returned it to her.

She said softly. "I'm not a thief. I want you to know that. Not really, I mean. I have this *compulsion*—this uncontrollable urge—to steal. I'm powerless to stop myself."

"Kleptomania?"

"Yes. I've been to several doctors, but they've been unable to cure me so far."

I shook my head in sympathy. "It must be terrible for you."

"Terrible," she agreed. "When my father learns of this, he'll have me put away in a hospital. He threatened to do that if I ever stole anything again."

I said, "Your father doesn't have to know what happened here today. There was no real harm done, actually. Mr. Stuyvesant will get his wallet and stickpin back. And I see no reason for causing the hotel unnecessary embarrassment through the publicity that will result if I report the incident."

Her face brightened hopefully. "Then—you're going to let me go?"

I took a long breath. "I suppose I'm too soft-hearted for the type of job that I have. Yes, I'm going to let you go. But you must promise me that you'll never set foot inside of the Hotel Poole again. If I ever see you here, I'll have to report you to the police."

"You won't!" she assured me earnestly. "I have an appointment with another doctor tomorrow morning. I feel sure I can be helped."

I nodded, then turned to stare through the lounge to where the guests were moving back and forth in the lobby. When I turned back again, the street door to the lounge was just closing and the young woman was gone.

I sat there for a short time, thinking about her. If she was a kleptomaniac, I decided, then I was the King of England. What she was, of course, was a professional pickpocket. I could tell that by her technique which was very skillful. She was also an extremely clever liar.

I smiled to myself and stood up and went out into the lobby again. But instead of resuming my position in the armchair, I made a sharp left and walked casually out of the hotel and on to Powell Street.

As I made my way through the afternoon crowds, my right hand rested lightly on the fat leather wallet and the diamond stickpin in my coat pocket. I found myself feeling a little sorry for the young woman. But just a little.

Because Andrew J. Stuyvesant had been *my* mark from the moment I first saw him entering the Hotel Poole that morning. I had waited three hours for him to come into the lobby. And I was just seconds away from bumping into him myself, when she came out of nowhere and grabbed his wallet and stickpin. So I figured I really had a right to them, after all.

TELLING ABOUT THE STORY. Complete each of the following statements by putting an *x* in the box next to the correct answer. Each statement tells something about the story.

1. The young woman
   - ☐ a. said that she was a friend of Andrew J. Stuyvesant.
   - ☐ b. gave Andrew J. Stuyvesant some things he had lost.
   - ☐ c. stole Andrew J. Stuyvesant's wallet and stickpin.

2. According to the man, he was
   - ☐ a. the manager of the hotel.
   - ☐ b. a waiter at the hotel.
   - ☐ c. the hotel detective.

3. The man told the young woman that he planned to
   - ☐ a. arrest her.
   - ☐ b. let her go.
   - ☐ c. call her father.

4. At the end of the story, we learn that the man
   - ☐ a. had just walked into the hotel lobby.
   - ☐ b. intended to rob Andrew J. Stuyvesant himself.
   - ☐ c. was planning to give up his life of crime.

WATCHING FOR NEW VOCABULARY WORDS. Answer the following vocabulary questions by putting an *x* in the box next to the correct response.

1. The young woman said that she could not control her compulsion to steal. A *compulsion* is
   - ☐ a. a very powerful impulse or urge.
   - ☐ b. a friend or companion.
   - ☐ c. information or knowledge.

2. The man shook his head in sympathy and said, "It must be terrible for you." Which of the following best defines the word *sympathy?*
   - ☐ a. hatred
   - ☐ b. greed
   - ☐ c. understanding

3. The woman's technique for picking pockets was very skillful. As used in this sentence, the word *technique* means
   - ☐ a. method.
   - ☐ b. promise.
   - ☐ c. purpose.

4. Although her face seemed innocent and shone with purity, she could not be trusted. The word *purity* means
   - ☐ a. guilt.
   - ☐ b. honesty.
   - ☐ c. thoughtfulness.

	× 5 =	
NUMBER CORRECT		YOUR SCORE

	× 5 =	
NUMBER CORRECT		YOUR SCORE

IDENTIFYING STORY ELEMENTS. Each of the following questions tests your understanding of story elements. Put an *x* in the box next to each correct answer.

1. What is the *setting* of this story?
   ☐ a. the lobby of an apartment building
   ☐ b. the main floor of a hotel
   ☐ c. a pool on Powell Street

2. What happened first in the *plot* of "A Dip in the Poole"?
   ☐ a. The man took the wallet and the stickpin from the bag.
   ☐ b. The young woman bumped into Mr. Stuyvesant and apologized.
   ☐ c. The young woman threatened to call the hotel manager.

3. The young woman and the man may both be *characterized* as
   ☐ a. helpful.
   ☐ b. truthful.
   ☐ c. liars.

4. What was the author's *purpose* in writing this story?
   ☐ a. to surprise and entertain the reader
   ☐ b. to teach or instruct the reader
   ☐ c. to change the reader's mind

SELECTING WORDS FROM THE STORY. Complete the following paragraph by filling in each blank with one of the words listed below. Each of the words appears in the story. Since there are five words and four blanks, one word in the group will not be used.

Experts _____ that homeowners
1

take some simple steps to protect their homes

against crime when they go on vacation. First,

make certain that all _____ and
2

windows are securely locked. Be sure to

_____ the delivery of mail, and ask
3

a neighbor to pick up newspapers or packages

that might be delivered. Set some timers so

that lights will go on at night. The

_____ of this is to make it less
4

obvious that the house is empty.

suggest   stop

doors

thief   purpose

	× 5 =	
NUMBER CORRECT		YOUR SCORE

	× 5 =	
NUMBER CORRECT		YOUR SCORE

THINKING ABOUT THE STORY. Each of the following questions requires you to think critically about the selection. Put an *x* in the box next to the correct answer.

1. We may infer that the young woman
   □ a. believed what the man told her.
   □ b. didn't believe what the man told her.
   □ c. had never stolen anything before.

2. We may infer that the man
   □ a. believed what the young woman told him.
   □ b. didn't believe what the young woman told him.
   □ c. had never stolen anything before.

3. It is likely that the young woman
   □ a. planned to return the articles she had taken.
   □ b. never returned to the Hotel Poole.
   □ c. saw a doctor the following morning.

4. The "twist" in this story is the fact that
   □ a. the "detective" was actually a thief.
   □ b. Mr. Stuyvesant didn't realize he had been robbed.
   □ c. the young woman was very beautiful.

Thinking More About the Story

- A pun is usually defined as "a play on words." According to a character in the story, the word *dip* is slang for "pickpocket." Tell why the story is called "A Dip in the Poole." Explain the pun in the title.
- "Two Dips in the Poole" might also have been an appropriate title. Explain why. How might this title have given away the ending of the story?
- The young woman promised the man that she would never come back to the hotel. Why do you think he wanted to make certain that she would never return? Think of at least two good reasons.

Use the boxes below to total your scores for the exercises.

☐ **T**elling About the Story
+
☐ **W**atching for New Vocabulary Words
+
☐ **I**dentifying Story Elements
+
☐ **S**electing Words from the Story
+
☐ **T**hinking About the Story
▼
☐ **S**core Total: Story 9

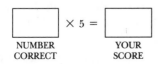

NUMBER CORRECT × 5 = YOUR SCORE

10. **The Padre's Neighbor**

by Manuela Williams Crosno

$\mathcal{E}$arly in the year 1870 there was a snowstorm about which the people of Los Hermanos still talk. All day snow fell, and wind whipped about the houses huddled in the mountain ridge.

It blew furiously against a man on the slopes who was attempting to ascend the long, steep climb to the village above. He was the only traveler in all that world of white.

The man had ridden out of Santa Fe early that morning in the face of the storm. From the distance, he had noticed that the mountains were covered with heavy, dark clouds. Now, as his horse slowly moved forward, the storm increased. The man urged the animal onward against the wind.

It was afternoon, but already darkness was approaching. Vanishing daylight made it difficult to see; soon the road was completely obscured.

The man dismounted and, having tied

his horse to a cedar tree, walked ahead in hopes of finding the trail. The blinding snow and bitter wind made it difficult to proceed. After a while, he struggled back to the place where he had tied his horse. The animal was gone! It had evidently pulled the rein free from the tree, and had drifted down the trail by which it had come.

For several minutes the man stood, looking about in bewilderment. In an effort to keep his hands warm, he beat them against his sides. All he could see was swirling snow, whipped about in angry puffs of freezing wind. A juniper tree twisted madly in the storm. The thought that he was lost in the eerie whiteness terrified him.

The man plodded forward determinedly, sometimes falling to his hands and knees in the snow, then picking himself up and pushing on.

Finally, he came to a place where the canyons widen and the ridge flattens out in a small, high plateau. It is a spot wedged against the peaks of the Sangre de Cristo mountains just west of Los Hermanos.

There was frost on his face and ice on his beard. The lids of his eyes were almost frozen shut. Just then, he came upon an open shed near the path. Making his way inside, he fell to the straw and lay there exhausted. He did not hear the goats in the opposite corner of the shed, bleating against the cold.

Father Jacobo Orosco of Los Hermanos stood in front of his warm fire and listened to the fury of the storm outside. He walked to a window, which was partly caked with snow, and looked out at the village. The storm had lessened, and in the whiteness the plaza looked like a painting.

The padre sighed and looked toward the fragile old building that served as a church. Barely visible through the swirling snow, it had at least weathered the storm.

Suddenly, Father Jacobo saw a horse moving slowly into the plaza. It was carrying a saddle!

The padre rushed outside, forcing the door closed behind him against the strength of the wind. Quickly, he summoned two men to set out in search of someone who had become lost in the storm.

In the middle of the night, the men from Los Hermanos came upon the traveler in the shed where he had strayed. So lifeless did he appear, it was as though the strong wind had lifted and then dropped him, like a sack of grain, on the straw. Quickly, they carried the man back to Father Jacobo.

At first, the padre thought that the man was dead, for his pulse was so feeble it could hardly be detected. After a while, there was a slight flicker of eyelids. The priest forced some tea between the man's tightly closed lips, and later gave him some soup. After several days, the stranger was finally able to move about.

The first thing he did was to shave off his beard. He was a tall man of about thirty-three, with dark hair, pale skin, and a long, thin face. There was a bitterness about the mouth—and great unhappiness in the deeply set eyes.

"What would those eyes look like?" Father Jacobo wondered, "if he ever smiled?"

The man gave his name as Stephen Bowen, but, other than that, revealed almost nothing about himself.

Father Jacobo inquired, "Why were you

coming here, to Los Hermanos, my son?"

There was a moment of silence. "I was lost, I guess." The answer was vague and evasive.

After that, Stephen Bowen did not mention from where he had come or why, and the padre did not inquire again. But Bowen's clothing bore the mark of an expensive London tailor. Father Jacobo, who had been to Europe, knew it well.

Since winter had come with full force, the road out of Los Hermanos would be blocked until May. No one could arrive or depart until then.

Bowen remained, and the people of Los Hermanos accepted this stranger whom their priest had befriended.

That winter, there were several incidents involving the man of mystery—incidents that gave Father Jacobo cause to reflect.

There were no doctors in Los Hermanos, although some of the good wives of the village knew many remedies that would cure common illnesses.

One day, a small boy who had broken his arm in a fall from a burro, was brought to the padre. Stephen Bowen looked at the boy, then carefully and professionally set the bone, bound the arm, and placed it in a sling.

Upon seeing the looks of surprise on the faces of those about him, Bowen said, "I am a physician—a *médico*."

That was just the first time that Bowen proved himself capable.

In February, Carlita, the small daughter of a family named Chávez, became seriously ill with a disease that Bowen diagnosed as scarlet fever. The people of Los Hermanos feared that the disease might spread, but under the care of the doctor, Carlita recovered and an epidemic was checked.

Before spring, the villagers came often to the *médico* for help. He spoke some Spanish and understood the people fairly well.

During that first winter, he became known as Esteban—the Spanish word for Stephen— and the name, Stephen Bowen, quickly disappeared.

With the springtime melting of snow, the trail was reopened, but Esteban, the *médico* of Los Hermanos, made no move to leave. Father Jacobo urged him to stay and arranged for him to live in a house next to his which had long been deserted and in need of repair. Little by little, over the course of the summer, the doctor remodeled the old house and made it quite livable.

There followed two happy years for Father Jacobo and the people of Los Hermanos. They all began to rely more and more on the services of the doctor. And although their *médico* never smiled, the lines of bitterness about his face began to soften.

Sometimes the padre, accompanied by the doctor, went on camping trips into the high mountains of the vast Sangre de Cristo range. There, the doctor confided to Father Jacobo that at Los Hermanos he had found peace, a peace he had never experienced in the world that was his before the snowstorm.

The doctor said no more, and the priest, as he had so often done, wondered who the doctor was and why he had chosen to stay at Los Hermanos.

Esteban built a campsite in the solitude of the mountains. Alone, he peered at the sky through pine needles, listened to the song of the wind in the forest, and slept beside the gentle splash of a mountain stream.

At this campsite one quiet evening, Esteban finally revealed to Father Jacobo how he had come to Los Hermanos.

"My brother and I were the only sons of a wealthy Englishman," said Esteban. "I studied medicine, while my brother became a lawyer and politician. My father believed very strongly in competition. All through his life, he set up contests between my brother and myself—contests in which I was not very interested.

"When our father died, we were left a large sum of money and a valuable piece of property. But a provision in the will stated that my brother and I were to engage in a contest to be agreed upon. The winner would be awarded the property."

Here, Esteban stopped. The padre saw the lines of fatigue on the face of the doctor. "It is late and you are tired," said the priest. "Perhaps tomorrow it will be easier to finish—"

"No," said Esteban, "let me continue. "One evening, my brother and I were sitting on a wharf waiting for the boat that would take us to Wales, where the property was located. I told my brother that I refused to engage in any sort of contest. I suggested that we divide the property equally instead."

Esteban shook his head, sadly. "But my brother disagreed. We quarreled angrily. I finally said I wanted none of the property, and left the wharf without waiting for the boat.

"The next morning, before dawn, a friend woke me to warn me that my brother had drowned in the channel. I was the chief suspect because several people had heard us quarreling! I knew I would be found guilty and thrown in jail—or possibly, hanged. I had very little time. My friend obtained a passport, and, disguised as him, I set sail on a freighter bound for Central America.

"I grew a beard, came north, and lived in Santa Fe under an assumed name. However, I told *you* my real name— Stephen Bowen.

"Soon a poster was brought by stage to Santa Fe. It contained a picture of me, a description, and the offer of a large reward. The detectives had been very clever in tracing me to the Southwest, although they did not specifically know where I was hiding. Even though I was innocent, there was no way I could prove it. I panicked!

"I mounted my horse and fled. I had heard of Los Hermanos—*the brothers!* How bittersweet to find refuge in a place with that name! With a small pack on my back, I rode out of Santa Fe. You know the rest."

The padre remained silent for a long time. Finally, he spoke. "I believe your story," he said softly. "Had you remained in England, you might not have been found guilty. However, what is done is done. But I am curious about something. Would you return to England if you knew that they had learned that you did not push your brother into the channel?"

"Would I return to England?" repeated the doctor. "I think you know the answer." For the first time that the padre could remember, the doctor smiled. "The man who arrived in the snowstorm—*he* would have returned." Esteban shook his head. "Not me."

The padre nodded. He understood this very well.

That spring, there was an even more serious outbreak of scarlet fever than before. Medicine was needed, for without it some children would surely die.

Rudolfo Garcia and his brother Josef volunteered to ride to Santa Fe to obtain the medicine. The padre accompanied them. Managing to break through the snowdrifts which blocked the road, they arrived at Santa Fe in the late afternoon. News quickly spread that Father Orosco from Los Hermanos was stopping at the parish.

The padre urged speed in the preparation of the medicine, so that they might return to Los Hermanos the following day. That night, a man came to the parish house and asked for Father Orosco.

"I will come quickly to my business," said the man, abruptly. "I am a detective. I have already wasted some time—and time and money are two things I do not waste.

"I have been making inquiries of persons from the villages around Santa Fe. Yours is the last. Perhaps you can help.

"I am looking for one Stephen Bowen," continued the detective. "He may be living in the area under an assumed name. There are those in England who seek him. That man was here a number of years ago—but all traces of him seem to have disappeared."

The speaker went on. "He is in his late thirties and may wear a beard. He studied to be a doctor, but it is not likely that he is practicing medicine. Here is a picture of him."

Father Orosco looked closely at the picture. He did not recognize it as that of Esteban—the *médico* of Los Hermanos.

"Well?" demanded the detective. "Have you seen this man?"

The padre faced his questioner squarely. There was a strange expression in the padre's eyes.

"Well?" pursued the detective.

"Yes," said the padre, "I have seen this man—in the blizzard of 1870." He paused. "The man you are looking for died in that blizzard."

The occasional cry of a bird could be heard as the padre and his companions ascended the mountains back to Los Hermanos—*the brothers!*

TELLING ABOUT THE STORY. Complete each of the following statements by putting an *x* in the box next to the correct answer. Each statement tells something about the story.

1. The men of Los Hermanos found Stephen Bowen
   □ a. hiding in Santa Fe.
   □ b. on a boat headed for Wales.
   □ c. lying exhausted in a shed.

2. Stephen Bowen was afraid that he would be found guilty of
   □ a. practicing medicine without a license.
   □ b. killing his brother.
   □ c. stealing his father's money.

3. Esteban helped the people of the village by
   □ a. repairing old houses.
   □ b. curing them of diseases.
   □ c. giving them money for food.

4. Father Orosco told the detective that
   □ a. he had never seen Stephen Bowen.
   □ b. he had seen Stephen Bowen in the blizzard of 1870.
   □ c. Stephen Bowen could be found in Los Hermanos.

WATCHING FOR NEW VOCABULARY WORDS. Answer the following vocabulary questions by putting an *x* in the box next to the correct response.

1. The man's pulse was so feeble, it could hardly be detected. The word *detected* means
   □ a. discovered.
   □ b. lost.
   □ c. improved.

2. As the daylight vanished it became difficult to see, and soon the road was completely obscured. Which of the following best defines the word *obscured*?
   □ a. clear
   □ b. hidden
   □ c. bumpy

3. An unusual provision in the will caused Bowen unhappiness. What is the meaning of the word *provision* as used in this sentence?
   □ a. a stock of food or supplies
   □ b. a requirement or condition
   □ c. an improvement or benefit

4. The detectives knew where Bowen had fled, but they could not determine specifically where he was hiding. Define the word *specifically*.
   □ a. exactly
   □ b. nearly
   □ c. swiftly

	× 5 =	
NUMBER CORRECT		YOUR SCORE

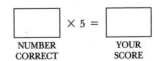

	× 5 =	
NUMBER CORRECT		YOUR SCORE

IDENTIFYING STORY ELEMENTS. Each of the following questions tests your understanding of story elements. Put an *x* in the box next to each correct answer.

1. "The Padre's Neighbor" is *set* in
   ☐ a. central England.
   ☒ b. northern Wales.
   ☐ c. the American Southwest.

2. What happened last in the *plot* of the story?
   ☐ a. Bowen told the priest about his father's will.
   ☐ b. The detective said that he was looking for Stephen Bowen.
   ☐ c. Father Orosco sent two men to look for someone lost in the storm.

3. Which sentence best *characterizes* the Stephen Bowen who first came to Los Hermanos?
   ☐ a. He seemed unhappy and said very little about himself.
   ☐ b. He was quite cheerful and made many close friends.
   ☐ c. He enjoyed telling the villagers about his past.

4. Which statement best expresses the *theme* of "The Padre's Neighbor"?
   ☐ a. An unhappy fugitive finds happiness.
   ☐ b. Never trust a stranger.
   ☐ c. It is impossible for a man to change.

☐ × 5 = ☐

NUMBER CORRECT   YOUR SCORE

SELECTING WORDS FROM THE STORY. Complete the following paragraph by filling in each blank with one of the words listed below. Each of the words appears in the story. Since there are five words and four blanks, one word in the group will not be used.

The city of Santa Fe is located high in the

_____ of New Mexico. Founded
          1

by the _____ in 1610, it is the
              2

oldest state capital in the United States. A

walk along the streets of the city will reveal

a _____ of beautiful houses and
        3

churches that were built by the early settlers

hundreds of years ago. Santa Fe is a city that

combines the _____ and the new.
                      4

window   mountains

number

Spanish   old

☐ × 5 = ☐

NUMBER CORRECT   YOUR SCORE

THINKING ABOUT THE STORY. Each of the following questions requires you to think critically about the selection. Put an *x* in the box next to the correct answer.

1. Evidence in the story suggests that the padre could honestly tell the detective that Stephen Bowen died because
   ☐ a. Bowen had become a new and very different man.
   ☐ b. Bowen was so weak, he nearly died.
   ☐ c. the detective had never seen Bowen.

2. We may infer that the detective
   ☐ a. didn't believe Father Orosco.
   ☐ b. stopped looking for Stephen Bowen.
   ☐ c. found Stephen Bowen later.

3. In Spanish, *Los Hermanos* means "the brothers." This is meaningful to the story because
   ☐ a. Stephen Bowen killed his brother at Los Hermanos.
   ☐ b. Bowen's brother had been planning to visit Los Hermanos.
   ☐ c. Bowen and Father Orosco "became brothers" at Los Hermanos.

4. It is reasonable to conclude that Stephen Bowen
   ☐ a. returned to England immediately.
   ☐ b. continued to live happily in the village.
   ☐ c. gave himself up to the detective.

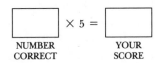

NUMBER CORRECT × 5 = YOUR SCORE

Thinking More About the Story

● For a long time, Stephen Bowen revealed almost nothing about himself. Then, one evening, Bowen told Father Orosco the details of his past. Why do you think that Bowen finally decided to tell the padre about himself?

● Bowen told Father Orosco that— even if it were safe to do so—he would not return to England. Why did Bowen feel this way?

● Do you think that the padre did the right thing when he told the detective that "The man you are looking for died in the blizzard"? Explain your answer.

Use the boxes below to total your scores for the exercises.

☐ + **T**elling About the Story

☐ + **W**atching for New Vocabulary Words

☐ + **I**dentifying Story Elements

☐ + **S**electing Words from the Story

☐ ▼ **T**hinking About the Story

☐ **S**core Total: Story 10

II. Dusk

by Saki

Norman Gortsby sat on a bench in the park, his back to the fence. Not far away, the rattle of traffic could be heard at a busy intersection. It was thirty minutes past six on an early March evening. Dusk had fallen over the scene—dusk brightened a bit by some faint moonlight and street lights.

The road and the sidewalk were empty. In the twilight, a few figures sat silently on the benches in the park. It was hard to distinguish them in the shadowy gloom in which they sat.

The scene pleased Gortsby and was well suited to his mood at that moment. To his mind, dusk was the hour of the defeated. It was the time when men and women who had fought and lost came forth. Then, with their dead hopes, and bent shoulders, and unhappy eyes, they might go unnoticed. At least they might pass unrecognized.

The wanderers in the dusk did not choose to have strangers stare at them. Therefore, they slipped quickly and silently through the paths, and made their way to benches. But beyond the sheltering screen of trees and shrubs in the park was a world of brilliant lights and noisy, rushing traffic. A blazing stretch of windows, one on top of the other, shone through the dark, illuminating it in spots.

Gortsby sat on his bench in the almost deserted park. He was in the mood to count himself among the defeated. Money problems he did not have. No, he was prosperous enough. He had failed in another ambition —in a matter of love. Now, heartsore and unhappy, he silently observed his fellow wanderers as they went their ways in the dark stretches between the lamp lights.

On the bench by Gortsby's side sat an elderly gentleman who stared off into the distance. His clothes, while not shabby, were very nearly so. As he rose to go, Gortsby imagined him returning to a home where he was snubbed and paid no attention. Or perhaps he went to some bleak lodging house where his ability to pay the rent bill was the only source of interest he inspired.

The elderly gentleman vanished slowly into the shadows, and his place on the bench was taken almost immediately by a young man. This man was fairly well dressed, but hardly more cheerful than the other. As if to clearly show that things were going badly with him, the newcomer muttered an angry curse as he flung himself into the seat.

"You don't seem to be in a very good mood," said Gortsby, since he judged that he was expected to notice the young man's behavior.

The young man turned to him, saying rather heatedly, "You wouldn't be in a good mood either, if you were in the fix I'm in. I've done the silliest thing I've ever done in my life."

"Yes?" said Gortsby.

"I traveled here this afternoon intending to stay at the Hollings Hotel. But when I got there, I found it had been torn down to make room for an office building. The taxi driver recommended another hotel which was some way off, and I went right there. I had just

sent a letter to my office giving them my address, and then I went out to buy some soap. I'd forgotten to pack any, and I hate using hotel soap. Then I strolled about a bit and did some window shopping.

"But when I got ready to go back to the hotel, I suddenly realized that I didn't remember its name, or even what street it was on. That's a nice situation for a fellow who hasn't any friends or relatives in this city! Of course I can send a telegram to my office for the address, but they won't be in until tomorrow morning. Meanwhile, I'm without any money. I left my room with a dollar bill to buy the soap. And here I am wandering about with just some loose change in my pocket and nowhere to go for the night."

There was a long pause after the story had been told. "I suppose you think I've spun you a rather impossible tale," said the young man, finally.

"Not at all impossible," said Gortsby slowly. "I remember doing the same sort of thing some years ago in a foreign city. And on that occasion there were two of us, which made it more remarkable. Luckily, we remembered the hotel was on a canal, and when we found the canal we were able to make our way back to the hotel."

The youth's face brightened at hearing this. Then he said, "You know in a foreign city, I wouldn't mind so much. One could go to the Embassy and get some help. Here in your own country, it's somewhat more difficult if you get into a fix. Unless I can get some decent fellow to swallow my story and lend me some money, I seem likely to spend the night out on the streets."

He looked straight at Gortsby as he made

this remark. His look seemed to suggest that Gortsby possessed the decency required.

"Of course," said Gortsby after a while, "the weak point in your story is that you can't produce the soap."

The young man felt rapidly in the pockets of his overcoat, and then jumped to his feet.

"I must have lost it," he said.

"To lose a hotel and a bar of soap on the same afternoon seems unusually careless," said Gortsby. But the young man hardly waited to hear the end of the remark. He hurried off quickly down the path, head held high, as though to protect his wounded pride.

"That was really a pity," thought Gortsby. "Going out to buy the soap was the one convincing touch in the whole story. And yet it was just that little detail that did him in. If he had thought ahead and provided himself with a bar of soap—something neatly wrapped in a little bag—he would certainly have succeeded. In his line of work, genius consists of paying attention to the smallest details."

With that thought in mind, Gortsby rose to go. As he did so, something of concern caught his eye. Lying by the side of the bench was a small oval package. Judging by its size and shape and by the paper in which it was wrapped—that of a local drug store—it could be nothing else but a bar of soap. It had evidently fallen out of the young man's overcoat pocket when he threw himself down on the bench.

A moment later Gortsby was rushing up and down in the dusk, searching for the young man in the overcoat.

He had nearly given up, when he saw the object of his quest. The young man was leaning against a railing, apparently making up

his mind whether or not to leave the park. He turned around sharply when he saw Gortsby waving.

"The important witness to the truthfulness of your story has turned up," said Gortsby. He held out the bar of soap. "It must have slipped out of your coat pocket when you sat down on the seat. I saw it on the ground after you left."

Gortsby paused for a moment, then continued. "You must excuse my not believing you. But your story, I think you'll agree, left something to be desired. However, now that the soap has turned up, my doubts have been erased. If a loan will be of any use to you, I think I can assist."

With that, Gortsby drew his wallet from his pocket and proceeded to count out a number of bills which he placed in the young man's hand.

"Here is my card with my address," continued Gortsby. "You may return the money any day this week. And here is the soap. Don't lose it again. It's been a good friend to you."

"Lucky thing for me your finding it," said the youth. And then, his voice nearly breaking, he blurted out a word or two of thanks, and fled quickly from the park.

"Poor boy—he nearly broke down," said Gortsby to himself. "I can see why, too. His relief must have been great. It's a lesson to me not to be too quick in judging situations."

As Gortsby made his way back to the bench where the entire incident had begun, he saw a man in nearly shabby clothes poking and peering beneath it and around it. Gortsby recognized him as the elderly gentleman who had been sitting there earlier.

"Have you lost anything, sir?" he asked.

"Yes, a bar of soap."

TELLING ABOUT THE STORY. Complete each of the following statements by putting an *x* in the box next to the correct answer. Each statement tells something about the story.

1. The young man told Gortsby that he
   ☐ a. couldn't find his hotel.
   ☐ b. had lost his wallet in a taxi.
   ☐ c. planned to spend the night at a friend's house.

2. At first, Gortsby didn't believe the young man's story because
   ☐ a. it could not possibly have happened.
   ☐ b. he knew that the young man was a liar.
   ☐ c. the young man didn't have the soap.

3. Gortsby gave the young man
   ☐ a. some loose change.
   ☐ b. a card with his address.
   ☐ c. the name of a nearby hotel.

4. The elderly gentleman told Gortsby that he had
   ☐ a. found a bar of soap.
   ☐ b. lost a bar of soap.
   ☐ c. no friends or relatives in the city.

WATCHING FOR NEW VOCABULARY WORDS. Answer the following vocabulary questions by putting an *x* in the box next to the correct response.

1. He finally found the object of his quest. The word *quest* means
   ☐ a. search.
   ☐ b. lamp.
   ☐ c. fortune.

2. Gortsby imagined the gentleman returning to a home where he was snubbed or paid no attention. What is the meaning of the word *snubbed*?
   ☐ a. ignored
   ☐ b. helped
   ☐ c. consulted

3. In the dim light, it was hard to distinguish the figures. As used in this sentence, the word *distinguish* means
   ☐ a. praise or honor.
   ☐ b. see or recognize.
   ☐ c. give or pay.

4. Gortsby did not have money problems—he was prosperous enough. Which of the following best defines the word *prosperous*?
   ☐ a. poor or penniless
   ☐ b. worried or troubled
   ☐ c. well-to-do or successful

☐ × 5 = ☐

NUMBER
CORRECT

YOUR
SCORE

☐ × 5 = ☐

NUMBER
CORRECT

YOUR
SCORE

IDENTIFYING STORY ELEMENTS. Each of the following questions tests your understanding of story elements. Put an *x* in the box next to each correct answer.

1. When is the story *set?*
   □ a. in the morning on a day in winter
   □ b. about three o'clock on a summer afternoon
   □ c. thirty minutes past six on a March evening

2. What happened last in the *plot* of "Dusk"?
   □ a. Gortsby saw the elderly gentleman looking for something.
   □ b. Gortsby placed some money in the young man's hand.
   □ c. The young man angrily flung himself onto the bench.

3. Which line of *dialogue* indicates that Gortsby found the soap?
   □ a. "To lose a hotel and a bar of soap on the same afternoon seems unusually careless."
   □ b. "The important witness to the truthfulness of your story has turned up."
   □ c. "Of course, the weak point of your story is that you can't produce the soap."

4. The *narrator* of "Dusk" is
   □ a. the author.
   □ b. Norman Gortsby.
   □ c. the young man.

□ × 5 = □

NUMBER CORRECT   YOUR SCORE

SELECTING WORDS FROM THE STORY. Complete the following paragraph by filling in each blank with one of the words listed below. Each of the words appears in the story. Since there are five words and four blanks, one word in the group will not be used.

   It is difficult to say exactly when soap was invented. However, it is believed that soap has been in use for thousands of

_____ . Evidence suggests that
          1

the ancient Babylonians, Egyptians, and

Romans made use of _____ . We
                              2

_____ that early American settlers
          3

used soap. They boiled kitchen grease with

lye to _____ their soap.
                  4

know   produce

soap

park   years

□ × 5 = □

NUMBER CORRECT   YOUR SCORE

THINKING ABOUT THE STORY. Each of the following questions requires you to think critically about the selection. Put an *x* in the box next to the correct answer.

1. We may infer that the young man
   - ☐ a. was a stranger to the city.
   - ☐ b. made up the story about the hotel and the soap.
   - ☐ c. actually became lost after he bought the soap.

2. Probably, the young man told Gortsby his story
   - ☐ a. because he was lonely.
   - ☐ b. because he was so upset.
   - ☐ c. to obtain money.

3. It is reasonable to assume that
   - ☐ a. Gortsby never heard from the young man again.
   - ☐ b. the young man eventually paid back the money to Gortsby.
   - ☐ c. the young man used the money to check into a hotel.

4. How do you think Gortsby felt following the conclusion of the story?
   - ☐ a. pleased that he had helped a stranger in need
   - ☐ b. sorry that he had doubted the stranger's story
   - ☐ c. foolish or tricked

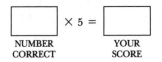

	× 5 =	
NUMBER CORRECT		YOUR SCORE

Thinking More About the Story

- Gortsby was probably not the first person to hear the young man's tale of woe. It is likely that the young man told others this story before. Explain why you agree or disagree with this statement.
- Even if the young man's story had been true, Gortsby should not have given him any money. Do you agree? Give reasons to support your opinion.
- This story is called "Dusk." Why? Think of another appropriate title for the selection. Explain your choice.

Use the boxes below to total your scores for the exercises.

	Telling About the Story
+	
	Watching for New Vocabulary Words
+	
	Identifying Story Elements
+	
	Selecting Words from the Story
+	
	Thinking About the Story
▼	
	Score Total: Story 11

12. The Sin of Madame Phloi

by Lilian Jackson Braun

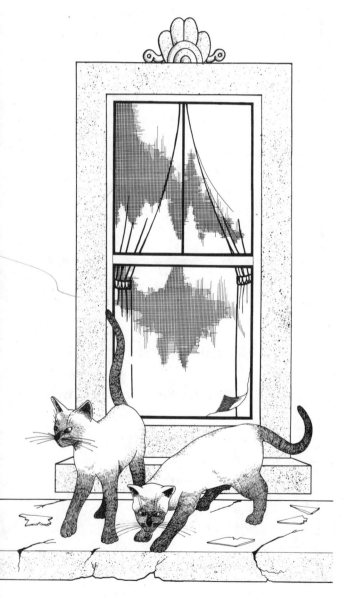

*F*rom the very beginning Madame Phloi felt an instant dislike for the man who moved into the apartment next door. He was fat, and his trouser cuffs had the odor of fire hydrant.

They met for the first time in the elevator as it lurched up to the tenth floor of the old building which was once fashionable. Madame Phloi had been out for a stroll in the city park, chewing grass and chasing butterflies. As she and her companion stepped on the elevator for the slow ride upward, the car was already half filled with the new neighbor.

"Get that cat away from me!" the fat man roared, stamping his feet at Madame Phloi. Madame Phloi's companion pulled on the leash. There was no need, though. Madame Phloi, with one leap, had retreated to a safe corner of the elevator.

"Don't you like cats?" asked the gentle voice at the other end of the leash.

"Filthy, sneaky beasts," the fat man said with a snarl. "The last place I lived at, some lousy cat got into my room and ate my parakeet."

"I'm sorry to hear that. Very sorry. But you don't need to worry about Madame Phloi and Thapthim. They never leave the apartment except on a leash."

"You got TWO cats? That's just fine! Keep 'em away from me, or I'll break their rotten necks."

And with the long black box he was carrying, the fat man lunged at Madame Phloi, who sat tensely in her corner.

Not until she was safely home in her modest apartment did she relax. She walked stiff-legged to the sunny spot on the carpet where Thapthim was sleeping, and licked the top of his head.

This drowsy, amiable creature—her son—was a puzzle to Madame Phloi, who was very high-spirited herself. She didn't try to understand him. She merely loved him.

Thapthim was lovable, to be sure. He had a face like a beautiful flower and large blue eyes, tender and trusting. He came when he was called. And when he was told to get down, he got down.

His parent, Madame Phloi, disapproved of this uncatly conduct. It indicated a certain lack of character which would lead to nothing good. According to Madame Phloi, when human hands reached out, the catly thing to do was to bound away and lead them a chase, before allowing oneself to be caught and cuddled. But Thapthim greeted any friendly gesture by rolling over and purring.

Until the fat man and his black box moved in next door, Madame Phloi had never known an unfriendly soul. She had two human companions in her tenth-floor apartment. They were very pleasant and genial creatures. One was an easy mark for between-meal snacks. A tap on his ankle always produced a spoonful of cottage cheese. The other obliged whenever Madame Phloi wished to have her fur or belly stroked.

Life was not all love and cottage cheese, however. Madame Phloi had her regular work. She was official watcher and listener for the household.

There were six windows that needed watching because a wide ledge ran around the building. It was right against the tenth-floor windowsills, and was a walkway for pigeons. They strutted along and ignored Madame Phloi, who sat on the sill and watched them through the window screen.

While watching was a daytime job, listening was done after dark. Madame Phloi listened for noises in the walls. She heard termites chewing and sometimes the ancient plaster cracking.

One evening, shortly after the incident in the elevator, Madame Phloi was listening when the fat man's voice burst through the wall like thunder.

"Look what you done!" he bellowed. "Get back in your cage before I brain you."

There was a frantic beating of wings.

"Get off my fiddle, or I'll bash your head in."

This threat brought only a torrent of chirping.

"Shut up, you stupid cluck! Shut up and get back in your cage, or I'll . . ."

There was a crash, and after that all was quiet except for an occasional pitiful "Peep!"

Madame Phloi was fascinated. Indeed, she hardly bothered to turn her head when the friendly window washer entered.

"Hi, kitty," he said in a musical voice. "Charlie's gotta take out that screen. Here, I brought you some cheese."

He held out a modest offering of cheese, and Madame Phloi investigated it. Unfortunately it was the wrong kind, and she rejected it.

"Mighty fussy cat," Charlie laughed.

"Well, now, you stay there and watch Charlie clean this here window. Don't you go jumpin' out on the ledge, because Charlie ain't runnin after you. No sir! That old ledge, she's startin' to crumble. Someday them pigeons'll stamp their feet hard, and down it'll go. Hey, look at the broken glass out here. Somebody busted a window. This screen, she's comin' apart, too. Whole buildin' seems to be crackin' up."

It was then that Madame Phloi noticed the tiny opening in the screen. Every opening, no matter how small, was a temptation. She had to prove she could wriggle through any tight space, whether there was a good reason or not.

She waited until Charlie had left the apartment before she began pushing at the screen with her nose. Inch by inch the rusted mesh ripped away from the frame until the whole corner formed a loose flap. Madame Phloi slithered through. For the first time in her life she found herself on the ledge. She gave a delighted shudder.

The ledge was about two feet wide. To its edge Madame Phloi moved warily, nose down and tail high. Ten stories below there were moving objects, but nothing of interest, she decided. Urged on by curiosity, she ventured in the direction of the fat man's apartment.

His window stood open and was without a screen. Madame Phloi peered in politely. There, sprawled on the floor, was the fat man himself, sleeping. In a dark corner of the room, a bird suddenly fluttered and squawked, and the fat man awoke.

"Shcrrff! Get out of here!" he shouted, struggling to his feet.

In three leaps Madame Phloi crossed the ledge back to her own window and pushed herself through the screen to safety. She looked back to see if the fat man might be chasing her and was reassured that he wasn't.

Madame Phloi made two more trips to the ledge and eventually convinced Thapthim to join her.

Together they peered over the edge at the world below. The sense of freedom was wonderful. They rolled over and over on the ledge, unconcerned about the long drop below them.

Suddenly Madame Phloi scrambled to her feet and crouched in a defensive position. The fat man was leaning from his window.

"Here, kitty, kitty," he was saying in a high, false voice. He was offering a bit of food in a saucer. Madame Phloi froze. But Thapthim turned his beautiful trusting eyes on the stranger and began advancing along the ledge. Purring, and waving his tail cordially, he walked into the trap. It all happened in a matter of seconds. The saucer was drawn back, and a long black box was swung at Thapthim like a baseball bat. It swept him off the ledge and into space. He was silent as he fell.

When the family came home, they knew at once something was wrong. No one greeted them at the door. Madame Phloi hunched on the windowsill staring at a hole in the screen, and Thapthim was not to be found.

"Look at the screen!" cried one voice.

"I'll bet he got out on the ledge."

"Can you lean out and look? Be careful."

"You hold Phloi."

"Do you see Thapthim?"

"Not a sign of him! There's a lot of glass scattered around, and the window's broken next door."

"Do you suppose that man . . . ? I feel sick."

"Don't worry. We'll find him."

"There's the doorbell! Maybe someone's bringing him home."

It was Charlie standing at the door. He fidgeted uncomfortably. " 'Scuse me, folks," he said. "You missin' one of your kitties?"

"Yes! Have you found him?"

"Poor little guy," said Charlie. "I found him lyin' right under your windows—where the bushes are thick."

"He's dead!" a voice moaned.

"Yes, ma'am. That's a long way down."

"Where is he now?"

"I got him down in the basement, ma'am. I'll take care of him real nice. I don't think you'd want to see the poor guy."

Still Madame Phloi stared at the hole in the screen and waited for Thapthim. From time to time she checked the other windows, just to be sure. As time passed and he did not return, she looked behind the radiators and under the bed. She sniffed all around the front door. Finally she stood in the middle of the living room and called loudly in a high-pitched, wailing voice.

The living room window was now tightly closed. But the following day, after she was left by herself in the apartment, Madame Phloi went to work on the bedroom screens. One was new and sturdy. But the second screen was slightly torn. She was soon making her way through a slight rip and was edging out onto the ledge.

She picked her way through the broken glass and approached the spot where Thapthim had vanished. And then it all happened again. There he was—the fat man—reaching forth with a saucer.

"Here, kitty, kitty."

Madame Phloi hunched down and backed away.

"Kitty want some milk?" It was that ugly false voice. But she didn't run home this time. She crouched there on the ledge, a few inches out of reach.

"Nice kitty. Nice kitty."

Madame Phloi crept with caution toward the saucer in the outstretched hand. The fat man extended another hand and snapped his fingers as one would call a dog.

Madame Phloi retreated just a bit.

"Here, kitty. Here, kitty," he cooed, leaning farther out. But he softly muttered, "You dirty sneak. I'll get you if it's the last thing I ever do. Comin' after my bird, weren't you?"

Madame Phloi recognized danger. Her ears went back and her whiskers curled, as she hugged the ledge.

A little closer she moved, and the fat man made a grab for her. She took one step back, keeping her unblinking eyes on his sweating face. He was slyly putting the saucer aside, she noticed, and edging farther out of the window.

Once more she advanced almost into his grasp, and again he lunged at her with both powerful arms.

Madame Phloi leaped lightly aside.

"This time I'll get you, you stinkin' cat," he cried. And raising one knee to the windowsill, he threw himself at Madame Phloi. As she slipped through his fingers, he landed on the ledge with all his weight.

A section of it crumbled beneath him. He bellowed, clutching at the air. The fat man was not silent as he fell.

As for Madame Phloi, she was later found on her living-room carpet, innocently washing her fine brown tail.

TELLING ABOUT THE STORY. Complete each of the following statements by putting an *x* in the box next to the correct answer. Each statement tells something about the story.

1. The man who moved into the apartment next door
   ☐ a. loved cats.
   ☐ b. hated cats.
   ☐ c. was very friendly.

2. Madame Phloi had the job of
   ☐ a. tasting new foods for the family.
   ☐ b. watching and listening for the family.
   ☐ c. scaring away unwelcome strangers.

3. The fat man tricked Thapthim by offering him
   ☐ a. a rubber ball.
   ☐ b. a spoonful of cottage cheese.
   ☐ c. some food in a saucer.

4. At the end of the story, Madame Phloi
   ☐ a. felt sorry for the fat man.
   ☐ b. became friendly with the fat man.
   ☐ c. caused the fat man to fall on the ledge.

WATCHING FOR NEW VOCABULARY WORDS. Answer the following vocabulary questions by putting an *x* in the box next to the correct response.

1. Since Madame Phloi did not like the treat Charlie offered her, she rejected it. Which expression best defines the word *rejected?*
   ☐ a. refused to take
   ☐ b. accepted gratefully
   ☐ c. inspected closely

2. Madame Phloi's human companions were very pleasant and genial creatures. What is the meaning of the word *genial?*
   ☐ a. friendly
   ☐ b. unfriendly
   ☐ c. lucky

3. Charlie fidgeted uncomfortably as he announced that Thapthim was dead. The word *fidgeted* means
   ☐ a. sat silently.
   ☐ b. moved about uneasily.
   ☐ c. laughed or joked.

4. Madame Phloi slithered through a small opening in the screen. What is the meaning of the word *slithered?*
   ☐ a. dropped
   ☐ b. slid
   ☐ c. leaped

	× 5 =	
NUMBER CORRECT		YOUR SCORE

	× 5 =	
NUMBER CORRECT		YOUR SCORE

IDENTIFYING STORY ELEMENTS. Each of the following questions tests your understanding of story elements. Put an *x* in the box next to each correct answer.

1. Where is "The Sin of Madame Phloi" *set*?
   ☐ a. in an elevator
   ☐ b. in an apartment house
   ☐ c. in a basement

2. What happened last in the *plot* of the story?
   ☐ a. The fat man warned Madame Phloi's companion to keep the cats away from him.
   ☐ b. The fat man threw himself at Madame Phloi.
   ☐ c. Thapthim waved his tail and advanced along the ledge toward the stranger.

3. Which group of words best *characterizes* Madame Phloi?
   ☐ a. high-spirited, fussy, proud
   ☐ b. drowsy, friendly, modest
   ☐ c. foolish, trusting, dull

4. Select the sentence which best expresses the *theme* of the story
   ☐ a. Cats make excellent pets.
   ☐ b. A cat is punished for committing a crime.
   ☐ c. A cat gains revenge on an enemy.

SELECTING WORDS FROM THE STORY. Complete the following paragraph by filling in each blank with one of the words listed below. Each of the words appears in the story. Since there are five words and four blanks, one word in the group will not be used.

Have you ever seen two high-spirited

kittens playing together? One kitten will

_____ down in wait for the other
         1

to pass by. Then it will suddenly

_____ up as though attacking an
         2

enemy. The other kitten will arch its back,

puff itself up, and begin _____
                                    3

toward the other in an attempt to frighten

it. By _____ attacking each other
              4

in play, kittens learn how to fight and how

to protect themselves.

advancing   leap

crouch

musical   innocently

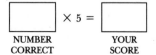

NUMBER
CORRECT   YOUR
SCORE

NUMBER
CORRECT   YOUR
SCORE

THINKING ABOUT THE STORY. Each of the following questions requires you to think critically about the selection. Put an *x* in the box next to the correct answer.

1. This story suggests that cats
   - ☐ a. think much the way that human beings do.
   - ☐ b. have better memories than people do.
   - ☐ c. are not very smart.

2. It may be said that Thapthim lost his life because he
   - ☐ a. took Madame Phloi's advice.
   - ☐ b. was too friendly and trusting.
   - ☐ c. was not curious enough.

3. The long, black object that the fat man swung at Thapthim was probably a
   - ☐ a. baseball bat.
   - ☐ b. golf club.
   - ☐ c. violin case.

4. It is likely that no one ever discovered
   - ☐ a. exactly who the fat man was.
   - ☐ b. the part that Madame Phloi played in her neighbor's death.
   - ☐ c. which foods Madame Phloi liked best.

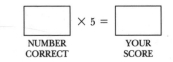

	× 5 =	
NUMBER CORRECT		YOUR SCORE

Thinking More About the Story

- At the end of the story, Madame Phloi "got even" with the fat man. Do you think that he deserved his fate? Give the reasons for your answer.
- Madame Phloi did not approve of Thapthim's "uncatly conduct" which she felt "would lead to nothing good." Explain how this proved to be the case.
- This story is called "The Sin of Madame Phloi." What was Madame Phloi's "sin"? What does the title seem to suggest?

Use the boxes below to total your scores for the exercises.

☐	**T**elling About the Story
+	
☐	**W**atching for New Vocabulary Words
+	
☐	**I**dentifying Story Elements
+	
☐	**S**electing Words from the Story
+	
☐	**T**hinking About the Story
▼	
☐	**S**core Total: Story 12

13. The Cop and the Anthem

by O. Henry

On his bench in Washington Square Park, Soapy moved uneasily. When sharp winds blow and dead leaves fall, and when Soapy moves uneasily on his bench in the park, then you may be certain that winter is near.

Soapy had become aware that the time had come for him to prepare for the coming cold winter season. And therefore he moved uneasily on his bench.

Three months in jail were what his heart most craved and desired. Three months of food, a bed to sleep on, and plenty of pleasant company—all away from the whistling winds of winter.

For years, a jail had been his winter quarters. While his more fortunate fellow New Yorkers bought tickets to Palm Beach and the Riviera each winter, Soapy always made humble arrangements for his annual journey to the jail. And now the time had come. On the previous night, three news-papers placed beneath his jacket, about his ankles, and over his lap, had failed to keep away the cold as he slept on his bench. So prison loomed timely in Soapy's mind.

Having made up his mind to go to jail, Soapy at once set about accomplishing this task. There were many easy ways of doing this. But the most pleasant was to dine lavishly at some expensive restaurant. Then, full to the brim, declare, "I'm broke," and let himself be handed over quickly and quietly to an officer of the law. An obliging judge would do the rest.

Soapy left his bench and strolled out of the park and up Broadway. He halted in front of a fancy restaurant and prepared to enter.

Soapy had confidence in himself. He was shaved, his jacket was decent, and his tie was neat and clean. If he could just reach a table in the restaurant without being seen, success would be his. The part of him that would show above the table would raise no suspicion in the waiter's mind. A roast duck, thought Soapy, would be just the thing to leave him filled and happy for the journey to his winter refuge.

But as Soapy set foot inside the restaurant, the head waiter's eyes fell on his ripped trousers and worn-out shoes. Strong and ready hands turned him around and led him in silence back to the street.

Soapy turned off Broadway. It seemed that his route to jail was not to be quite so pleasant. Still, there were other ways of achieving his goal.

At a corner of Sixth Avenue, Soapy paused in front of a beautiful store window. Inside, elegant and expensive wares were dis-played. Soapy picked up a rock and hurled it through the glass. In a moment people came running around the corner, a police-man in the lead. Soapy stood still, with his hands in his pockets, and smiled at the sight of the officer.

"Where's the man who did that?" inquired the officer, excitedly.

"Don't you think it might have been me?" said Soapy, cheerfully.

The policeman refused to even consider this. "People who smash windows," he said, "do not hang around to discuss it with the law. They take to their heels." Just then, the policeman saw a man halfway down the block running to catch a car. Drawing his club, he joined in the pursuit. With disgust in his heart, Soapy kept walking along— twice unsuccessful now.

On the opposite side of the street was a small luncheonette. It offered large portions at small prices. Soapy had no trouble enter-ing there. At a table he sat and ordered, and consumed steak, pancakes, doughnuts, and pie. When he was finished, Soapy signaled to the waiter.

"I don't have a single cent," said Soapy. "Now, get busy and call a cop. And don't keep a gentleman waiting."

"No cop for you," said the waiter. "Hey, Stanley, give me a hand."

An instant later, another waiter appeared. The two grabbed Soapy by his lapels and bounced him out onto the hard pavement. Soapy arose, every bone in his body aching, and slowly brushed the dust off his clothing. Arrest seemed just a rosy dream. Jail seemed very far away. A policeman on the corner laughed and walked down the street.

Soapy traveled five blocks more before another opportunity presented itself. This time it seemed to him a "cinch." A young and well dressed woman was standing in front of a store window. She gazed with great interest at the display of items inside. A large, serious-looking policeman stood just two doors away.

It was Soapy's plan to "make a pass" at the young woman. She would then promptly call the nearby cop. Soapy could almost feel the officer's hand on his arm—the hand that would assure him of three months in jail.

Soapy straightened his tie, set his hat at an angle, and moved slowly toward the young woman. He coughed loudly several times, smiled, and winked at her repeatedly. Out of the corner of his eye, Soapy saw that the policeman was watching him with interest.

The young woman moved away a few steps and again looked in the store window. Soapy, following boldly, stepped to her side, raised his hat and said, "Don't I know you from somewhere?"

The policeman was still looking. Soapy knew that the young woman had but to signal the policeman and he would practically be on his way to jail. Already he imagined he could feel the cozy warmth of the station house.

Soapy winked twice again and said slyly, "I say, Miss, haven't we met before?"

The young woman stared at him silently. Then a light came into her eyes. *"Yes,"* she said, "you're *Soapy.* You were pointed out to me at a benefit for charity which was held at the park."

She stretched out an arm to shake his hand. But Soapy, overcome with gloom, turned on his heels, and, walking quickly, made his way past the policeman. He seemed to be doomed to liberty.

Three blocks away in a drugstore he saw a well-dressed man paying for some items he had purchased. He had set his silk umbrella by the side of the counter as he reached for his wallet. Soapy stepped inside the store, grabbed the umbrella, and slowly walked off with it. The man in the drugstore followed Soapy hastily.

"Hey, that's my umbrella," he said, sternly.

"Oh, is it?" sneered Soapy. "Well, why don't you call a policeman? I took it. It's your umbrella. Why don't you call a cop? There's one on the corner."

The owner of the umbrella slowed his steps. Soapy did the same. The policeman looked curiously at the two of them.

"Of course," said the other man, "that is—well, you know how these mistakes happen. I—if it's your umbrella I hope you'll excuse me. I picked it up this morning in a restaurant. If you recognize it as yours, why—I hope you'll—"

The umbrella man walked quickly away. The policeman moved off to help an elderly man cross the street.

Soapy hurled the umbrella away angrily. He muttered insults about the police. Because he wanted to be arrested, they treated him as a king who could do no wrong.

At an unusually quiet corner Soapy came to a halt. Here was an old church. Through a stained-glass window a soft light glowed. Organ music drifted sweetly out to Soapy's ears.

The moon above was unusually brilliant and clear. All was peaceful, serene. Birds twitted sleepily. For a little while the scene might have been of a country churchyard. Soapy stood against the iron fence listening to the music. It reminded him of the days when he was young.

The combination of the music, and the setting, and the thoughts of his youth moved Soapy very much. They brought about a sudden and wonderful change in him. He realized with horror how far he had fallen. In an instant, he made a decision. He would pull himself together. He would make a man of himself again. There was still time. He would pursue his youthful dreams and ambitions and make them come true.

The solemn but sweet organ notes had affected him deeply. Tomorrow he would go to the downtown business district and find work. A man he knew had once offered him a job. He would find him tomorrow and ask for the position. He would be somebody in the world. He would—

Soapy felt a hand on his arm. He looked quickly around into the face of a policeman.

"What are you doing here?" asked the officer.

"Nothing," said Soapy.

"Then come along," said the policeman.

"Three months in jail for loitering," said the judge in the police court the next morning.

TELLING ABOUT THE STORY. Complete each of the following statements by putting an *x* in the box next to the correct answer. Each statement tells something about the story.

1. Soapy wanted to spend three months in jail because he
   - ☐ a. felt guilty about a crime.
   - ☐ b. needed a quiet place where he could reflect about his life.
   - ☐ c. wished to spend the winter in a warm place.

2. Soapy was turned away at a fancy restaurant because
   - ☐ a. he had broken the window with a rock.
   - ☐ b. he had not made a reservation.
   - ☐ c. the head waiter saw Soapy's ripped trousers and worn-out shoes.

3. As he listened to the church music and thought about his youth, Soapy decided to
   - ☐ a. make something of his life.
   - ☐ b. try once more to get thrown in jail.
   - ☐ c. spend the next few months living in the park.

4. The policeman didn't believe Soapy smashed the window because Soapy
   - ☐ a. was nowhere near the scene of the crime.
   - ☐ b. admitted it so willingly.
   - ☐ c. had no reason to break the window.

	× 5 =	
NUMBER CORRECT		YOUR SCORE

WATCHING FOR NEW VOCABULARY WORDS. Answer the following vocabulary questions by putting an *x* in the box next to the correct response.

1. Three months in jail were what Soapy craved and desired. Which expression best defines the word *craved?*
   - ☐ a. disliked greatly
   - ☐ b. wanted urgently
   - ☐ c. seldom thought about

2. It was very pleasant to dine lavishly at some expensive restaurant. The word *lavishly* means
   - ☐ a. fully or abundantly.
   - ☐ b. hurriedly or quickly.
   - ☐ c. sadly or sorrowfully.

3. Soapy ordered and consumed steak, pancakes, doughnuts, and pie. As used in this sentence, the word *consumed* means
   - ☐ a. decided against.
   - ☐ b. ate completely.
   - ☐ c. thought about.

4. As Soapy listened to the music, all was peaceful and serene. What is the meaning of the word *serene?*
   - ☐ a. loud
   - ☐ b. quiet
   - ☐ c. unusual

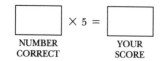

	× 5 =	
NUMBER CORRECT		YOUR SCORE

IDENTIFYING STORY ELEMENTS. Each of the following questions tests your understanding of story elements. Put an *x* in the box next to each correct answer.

1. Which sentence best *characterizes* Soapy?
   - ☐ a. He was well-dressed and often ate at expensive restaurants.
   - ☐ b. He had an excellent job in the downtown business district.
   - ☐ c. He didn't have a job and spent his nights sleeping on a park bench.

2. What happened last in the *plot* of the story?
   - ☐ a. A judge sentenced Soapy to three months in jail.
   - ☐ b. Soapy smiled and winked at a young woman.
   - ☐ c. Two waiters threw Soapy out into the street.

3. Judging by this story and "The Last Leaf" (page 17), what is O. Henry's *style?*
   - ☐ a. His stories contain no dialogue.
   - ☐ b. His stories contain many long, descriptive passages.
   - ☐ c. His stories conclude with a surprise ending.

4. What was the author's *purpose* in writing this story?
   - ☐ a. to instruct the reader
   - ☐ b. to entertain the reader
   - ☐ c. to change the reader's mind

	× 5 =	
NUMBER CORRECT		YOUR SCORE

SELECTING WORDS FROM THE STORY. Complete the following paragraph by filling in each blank with one of the words listed below. Each of the words appears in the story. Since there are five words and four blanks, one word in the group will not be used.

Alcatraz was once the most famous

_____ in the United States.
1

It is located on twelve acres of solid

_____ in San Francisco Bay. More
2

than one mile of water _____
3

between Alcatraz Island and the mainland.

In 1963, the federal government closed

Alcatraz because it was badly in need of

repair and became too _____ to
4

run. Today, Alcatraz is an interesting tourist

attraction.

arrested   expensive

prison

stretches   rock

	× 5 =	
NUMBER CORRECT		YOUR SCORE

THINKING ABOUT THE STORY. Each of the following questions requires you to think critically about the selection. Put an *x* in the box next to the correct answer.

1. What is amusing about this story is that
   □ a. Soapy realized there was still time to pursue his youthful dream.
   □ b. winter was coming and it was beginning to get cold.
   □ c. the moment Soapy changed his mind about going to jail, he was sent there.

2. At one point in the story, Soapy walked off with another man's umbrella. From the man's actions, we may infer that he
   □ a. paid a great deal of money for the umbrella.
   □ b. was given the umbrella as a gift.
   □ c. had stolen the umbrella from someone else.

3. How do you think Soapy felt when the young woman said that she knew him?
   □ a. shocked
   □ b. pleased
   □ c. worried

4. Based on this story, it is reasonable to conclude that O. Henry
   □ a. usually wrote about rich and famous people.
   □ b. didn't enjoy writing about city life.
   □ c. had an excellent sense of humor.

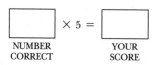

NUMBER
CORRECT   × 5 =   YOUR
SCORE

Thinking More About the Story

● An anthem may be defined as a song of praise or joy. Why do you think this story is called "The Cop and the Anthem"? Think of another title which is appropriate.
● If Soapy had not been sent to jail at the end of the story, do you think he would have changed his style of life? If so, how? What do you think Soapy will do after he is released from jail?
● Think of one more thing that Soapy might have done in order to be thrown in jail. Figure out a way to make the attempt unsuccessful.

Use the boxes below to total your scores for the exercises.

□
  +
Telling About the Story

□
  +
Watching for New Vocabulary Words

□
  +
Identifying Story Elements

□
  +
Selecting Words from the Story

□
  ▼
Thinking About the Story

□
Score Total: Story 13

97

14. The Man and the Snake

by Ambrose Bierce

*I*t was Harold Brayton's habit to read a bit before going to bed. And although he was a guest at the Drurings' house, he found it difficult to sleep without reading a few lines. Brayton moved to the bookcase in the guest room he was using and glanced over the books. One, in particular, caught his eye. It was an old volume whose aged leather jacket was cracking. It was entitled Morrison's *Marvels of Science.*

Brayton, who was a scientist and teacher himself, was curious to see what "marvels of science" passed for truth in old Morrison's day. He settled himself in a chair, flipped open the book, and came to the following passage:

> *The following is a fact, for many wise and learned people have reported it to be true. The eyes of the serpent have a magnetic quality. Whoever is drawn into its gaze will be unable to look away. Therefore NEVER stare into the eyes of a snake, or you will perish miserably by the creature's bite.*

Brayton smiled as he read this passage. "The only marvel in this matter," he said to himself, "is that the wise and learned people of Morrison's day should have believed such nonsense." Brayton shook his head as he muttered, "Imagine a snake's eyes having such power! Ridiculous!"

Brayton, however, could not help thinking about the words, because he was, after all, a man of thought. As he did, Brayton lowered the book without realizing he had done so. As soon as the volume had gone below the level of his eyes, something in a corner of the room caught his attention.

What he saw in the shadow under his bed was two small points of light, about an inch apart. They might have been reflections of something in the room. He gave them little thought and resumed his reading. After reading two paragraphs more, something inside him made him lower the book, and look again toward the shadow.

The points of light were still there. They seemed to have become brighter than before and shone with a greenish glow that he had not noticed before. He thought, too, that they might have moved just a bit—were somewhat nearer.

They were still too deep in the shadow to be clearly seen, and again he went back to his reading. Suddenly, something occurred to him which startled him and made him drop the book. He arose from the chair, bent over, and stared into the darkness beneath the bed. The points of light, it seemed to him, shone with even greater brightness now. His curiosity was now completely aroused. He came closer to the bed and peered under it.

He saw, in the shadow under the bed, the coils of a large serpent. The points of light were its eyes! Its head, which arose from the coils, was pointed straight toward him. The snake's eyes gazed at him. They looked deep into his own.

A snake in the bedroom of a house in the city is rather unusual. Therefore, an explanation for it is necessary. Harold Brayton, a scientist and teacher, had just returned to San Francisco from a trip to Europe where he had been doing research. He had gladly accepted the invitation of Dr. Druring, the distinguished scientist, to spend several days at his home.

Dr. Druring's house had undergone many changes over the years. One section or "wing" had been converted to a combination laboratory, museum, and zoo. It was here that Dr. Druring engaged in scientific study. He was particularly interested in reptiles such as snakes, although he had a large collection of lizards and turtles, as well. Druring's wife and daughter liked to call this section the "Snakery." Each occupant of the Snakery had its own well-protected compartment. Still, from time to time, one or two managed to escape, and showed up in some other part of the house.

Brayton was somewhat shocked and surprised when he first saw the snake. Beyond that he was not greatly affected. His first thought was to leave the room at once, and bring word of the serpent to Dr. Druring's attention.

Then Brayton paused. It occurred to him that to do this might make it appear that he was afraid—which he was not. He merely felt that the situation was awkward and absurd.

The snake was one of a species with which Brayton was not familiar. He could only guess at its length. The body, as far as he was able to see, was about as thick as his arm. In what way was the snake dangerous—if in any way at all? Was it poisonous? Could it choke a victim? He could not tell. He was not an expert on snakes.

If the snake was not dangerous, it was certainly annoying, or offensive. It was clearly out of place—a nuisance. It had no business being there.

What should he do? Brayton thought about the matter, then made a decision. He rose to his feet and got ready to back quietly away from the snake, without disturbing it, if possible. He would then head for the door. He knew that he could walk backward without any difficulty. Meanwhile, the snake's eyes glared evilly at him.

Brayton lifted his right foot to take a step backward. At that moment he felt reluctant, or unwilling, to do so.

"I am considered brave," he said. "Just because there is no one to witness it, shall I act like a coward?"

He put his right hand on the back of a chair to steady himself. As he did so, he said aloud, "Just the same, I am not so foolish as to act unwisely."

He attempted to take a step backward, but, much to his amazement, he found that his right foot refused to move. The result was the same when he tried the left foot. His hand was on the chair, grasping it tightly. All the while, the snake's head was still thrust

forward. The head had not moved. Its eyes glared at the man. They were like electric sparks, throwing off sparkling needles of light.

The man grew pale. He forced himself to take a step forward, and another. He dragged the chair, which suddenly slipped and fell to the ground with a crash.

The man uttered a groan. The snake had not made a sound nor moved. But its eyes were like two dazzling suns. They gave off rings of bright and vivid colors which floated toward him—then vanished like soap-bubbles.

He heard, somewhere, the continuous beating of drums. Then the drum-beats stopped, or rather became the distant roll of thunder. It seemed to him he saw—as though in a dream—a huge rainbow, and under its curve a giant serpent wearing a crown. The snake raised its head. . . .

Suddenly, something struck him a hard blow on his face and chest. He had fallen to the floor. He knew then that by this fall—by looking away from the eyes of the serpent—he had broken the spell that had held him. He felt certain that by making sure not to look at the snake again, he would be able to retreat. But the thought that the snake was just a few feet away from his head was more than he could bear. He lifted his head, stared again into the serpent's eyes, and was once more under its spell.

The snake had not moved. Its eyes now simply glowed. It was as if the creature knew it had triumphed and was enjoying its victory.

The man lay on the floor. He raised himself up partly on his elbows. His eyes were strained open to their fullest. Slowly he began to move. And every movement brought him closer to the serpent.

Dr. Druring and his wife sat in the library. The scientist was in a very good mood.

"I have just obtained," he said, "a wonderful example of the *ophiophagus.*"

"And what is the *ophiophagus?*" inquired Mrs. Druring.

"The *ophiophagus,*" he replied, "is a snake that swallows up other snakes."

"But how does it get the other snakes? By charming them, I suppose."

"Hardly," said Dr. Druring. "There is no truth at all to that silly idea that a snake has the power to cast a spell over other creatures."

The conversation was suddenly interrupted by a loud cry which rang through the silent house. Over and over it sounded. Almost before the echo of the last cry had died away the doctor was out of the room, springing up the stairs two steps at a time. In the hall in front of Brayton's room he met another guest. Together they rushed into the room. Brayton lay on the floor, dead. His eyes were wide open, and staring.

"He obviously died in a fit," said Dr. Druring, bending over the body. While Druring was in that position, he happened to look under the bed.

"Now how did this thing get in here?" he asked.

He reached under the bed, pulled out the snake and flung it away. It slid across the floor until it hit the wall where it lay without moving.

It was a stuffed snake. Its eyes were two glass marbles.

TELLING ABOUT THE STORY. Complete each of the following statements by putting an *x* in the box next to the correct answer. Each statement tells something about the story.

1. Harold Brayton read a passage which stated that
   □ a. most snakes are harmless.
   □ b. one should never show fear to a snake.
   □ c. it is dangerous to stare into the eyes of a snake.

2. When he first saw the snake, Brayton was
   □ a. amused and pleased.
   □ b. shocked and surprised, but not afraid.
   □ c. too frightened to speak.

3. When Brayton fell to the ground, he broke
   □ a. his foot.
   □ b. his arm.
   □ c. the spell he was under.

4. At the end of the story, the creature under the bed proved to be a
   □ a. poisonous snake.
   □ b. snake which could choke its victims.
   □ c. stuffed snake.

WATCHING FOR NEW VOCABULARY WORDS. Answer the following vocabulary questions by putting an *x* in the box next to the correct response.

1. Harold Brayton read a book which was entitled Morrison's *Marvels of Science.* In this sentence, the word *entitled* means
   □ a. allowed.
   □ b. owed.
   □ c. named.

2. After he saw the two points of light, Brayton resumed his reading and read two more paragraphs. Define the word *resumed.*
   □ a. flung away
   □ b. began again
   □ c. called out

3. Dr. Druring's house had undergone several changes; one section had been converted and was now a laboratory. The word *converted* means
   □ a. kept exactly the same.
   □ b. altered or made different.
   □ c. rented to guests.

4. The snake had no business being there, and was annoying, or offensive. Which of the following best defines the word *offensive?*
   □ a. bothersome or disturbing
   □ b. welcome or agreeable
   □ c. invited or requested

☐ × 5 = ☐
NUMBER CORRECT   YOUR SCORE

☐ × 5 = ☐
NUMBER CORRECT   YOUR SCORE

IDENTIFYING STORY ELEMENTS. Each of the following questions tests your understanding of story elements. Put an *x* in the box next to each correct answer.

1. "The Man and the Snake" is *set* in a
   ☐ a. house.
   ☐ b. museum.
   ☐ c. zoo.

2. What happened first in the *plot* of the story?
   ☐ a. Brayton discovered that he could not lift his feet.
   ☐ b. Dr. Druring rushed out of the room, and sprang up the stairs.
   ☐ c. Brayton peered under the bed and saw, in the shadow, the coils of a snake.

3. The *mood* of this story is
   ☐ a. humorous or comic.
   ☐ b. horrifying or ironic.
   ☐ c. light and amusing.

4. Select the sentence which best expresses the *theme* of "The Man and the Snake."
   ☐ a. It is better to be a live coward than a dead hero.
   ☐ b. Snakes are not as harmful as some people think they are.
   ☐ c. A man's vivid imagination brings about his destruction.

SELECTING WORDS FROM THE STORY. Complete the following paragraph by filling in each blank with one of the words listed below. Each of the words appears in the story. Since there are five words and four blanks, one word in the group will not be used.

Snakes do not have very good eyesight. The eyes of a snake are placed on either side of its _____₁_____ . Because of the _____₂_____ of its eyes, the snake can see over a wide area. However, it has great _____₃_____ seeing very far. The snake relies more on its inner ear and its tongue than on its _____₄_____ to gain information about its surroundings.

position   head

stairs

eyes   difficulty

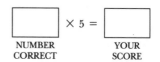

NUMBER CORRECT   × 5 =   YOUR SCORE

NUMBER CORRECT   × 5 =   YOUR SCORE

THINKING ABOUT THE STORY. Each of the following questions requires you to think critically about the selection. Put an *x* in the box next to the correct answer.

1. We may infer that Harold Brayton died of
   ☐ a. an old injury.
   ☐ b. a snake bite.
   ☐ c. fright.

2. Probably, the author provided the information about the "Snakery" to make the reader think that
   ☐ a. Dr. Druring was a very careful scientist.
   ☐ b. Brayton should not have accepted an invitation to be a guest at Dr. Druring's home.
   ☐ c. the snake under the bed was real.

3. If Brayton had *not* read the passage about the snake, it is likely that he would have
   ☐ a. been able to leave the room without difficulty.
   ☐ b. decided to attack the snake.
   ☐ c. experienced exactly the same fate.

4. Which of the following expressions best applies to this story?
   ☐ a. You can't teach an old dog new tricks.
   ☐ b. Don't leap out of the frying pan into the fire.
   ☐ c. The only thing we have to fear is fear itself.

	× 5 =	
NUMBER CORRECT		YOUR SCORE

Thinking More About the Story

- Sometimes, the power of suggestion can be very strong. Prove this statement by referring to the story.
- At one point in "The Man and the Snake," Brayton had difficulty moving his feet. What do you think caused this problem? Explain.
- Show how the snake's eyes played a very important role in this story. Why couldn't Brayton look away from the eyes?

Use the boxes below to total your scores for the exercises.

☐ +	**T**elling About the Story
☐ +	**W**atching for New Vocabulary Words
☐ +	**I**dentifying Story Elements
☐ +	**S**electing Words from the Story
☐ ▼	**T**hinking About the Story
☐	**S**core Total: Story 14

15. A Mother in Mannville

by Marjorie Kinnan Rawlings

The orphanage is high in the Carolina mountains. Sometimes in winter the snow is so deep that the institution is cut off from the villages below. Fog hides the mountain peaks. The snow swirls down the valleys. And the wind blows bitterly.

"Sometimes you can get frostbite on your face if it's really cold," said Jerry. "I have gloves," he added. "Some of the boys don't have any."

I was there in the autumn. I wanted quiet to do some writing. I rented a cabin that belonged to the orphanage, half a mile beyond the orphanage farm. When I took the cabin, I asked for a boy or a man to come and chop wood for the fireplace. The first few days were warm, and I found what wood I needed about the cabin. No one came, and I forgot about the order.

I looked up from my typewriter one late afternoon, a little startled. A boy stood at the door, and my dog was at his side and had not barked to warn me. The boy was probably twelve years old, but short for his age. He wore overalls and a torn shirt.

He said, "I can chop some wood today."

I said, "But I have a boy coming from the orphanage."

"I'm the boy."

"You? But you're small."

"Size don't matter chopping wood," he said. "Some of the big boys don't chop good. I've been chopping wood at the orphanage a long time."

"Very well," I said, a little annoyed. "There's the ax. Go ahead and see what you can do."

I went back to work and he began to chop. I suppose an hour and a half passed, for when I stopped typing and heard the boy's steps on the cabin stoop, the sun was setting behind the mountains.

The boy said, "I have to go to supper now. I can come again tomorrow evening."

I said, "I'll pay you now for what you've done," thinking I should probably have to insist on an older boy.

"Anything is all right."

We went together to the back of the cabin. An astonishing amount of solid wood had been cut.

"But you've done as much as a man," I said, "This is a splendid pile."

I looked at him, actually, for the first time. His hair was the color of corn and his eyes were very direct—gray with a shadowing of blue. I gave him some money.

"You may come back tomorrow," I said, "and thank you very much."

He looked at me, and at the money, and seemed to want to speak, but could not, and turned away.

"I'll split kindling tomorrow," he said. "You'll need kindling and medium wood, and some larger logs."

At daylight I was half awakened by the sound of chopping. When I left my bed in the cool morning, the boy had gone. A stack of kindling was piled neatly against the cabin wall.

He came again in the afternoon and worked until time to return to the orphanage. His name was Jerry. He was twelve years old, and he had been at the orphanage since he was four. I could picture him at four with the same—the word that comes to me is "integrity." It means honesty but it is more than honesty. The ax handle broke one day. Jerry said the woodshop at the orphanage would repair it. I brought money to pay for the job, and he refused it.

"I'll pay for it," he said. "I broke it. I brought the ax down careless."

"But no one hits accurately every time," I told him.

He stood behind his own work. He chose to do careful work, and if he failed, he took the responsibility.

And he did for me thoughtful, gracious things. He made a place near the fireplace to put kindling and medium-sized wood. A stone was loose on the path to the cabin. He dug a deeper hole and wedged it in, although he, himself, came by a different way.

He made excuses to come and sit with me. I suggested that the best time to visit was just before supper when I finished writing. He became friendly, of course, with my dog, Pat. When I went away for a weekend, I left Jerry in charge of the dog. I gave Jerry the dog whistle and the key to the cabin, and I left sufficient food. He was to come two or three times a day and let out the dog, and feed and exercise him.

I was supposed to return Sunday night, but fog filled the mountains so treacherously that I dared not drive at night. It was noon on Monday before I reached the cabin. The dog had been fed and cared for that morning. Jerry came early in the after-noon, anxious.

"They said nobody would drive in the fog," he said. "I came just before bedtime last night and you hadn't come. So I brought Pat some of my breakfast this morning. I wouldn't let anything happen to him."

"I was sure of that. I didn't worry."

"I thought you'd know."

That night he came in the darkness and knocked at the door.

"Come in, Jerry," I said, "if you're allowed to be away this late."

"I told maybe a story," he said. "I told them I thought you would want to see me."

"That's true," I assured him, and I saw he was relieved. "I want to hear about how you managed with the dog."

He sat by the fire with me and told me of their two days together. The dog lay close to him. And it seemed to me that the dog had brought the boy and me together, so that he felt that he belonged.

"You look a little bit like my mother," he said suddenly. "Especially in the dark, by the fire."

"But you were only four, Jerry, when you came here. Have you remembered how she looked, all these years?"

"My mother lives in Mannville," he said.

For a moment, finding that he had a mother shocked me as greatly as anything in my life. I was filled with a passionate anger that any woman should go away and leave her son. Especially a son like this one.

"Have you seen her, Jerry—lately?"

"I see her every summer. She sends for me."

I wanted to cry out, "Why are you not with her? How can she let you go away again?"

He said, "She comes up here from Mannville whenever she can. She doesn't have a job now."

His face shone in the firelight.

"You remember the suit I had on last Sunday?" He was clearly proud. "She sent me that for Christmas. The Christmas before that"—he drew a long breath, enjoying the memory—"she sent me a pair of skates."

"Roller skates?"

She had not, then, completely deserted or forgotten him. But why, I thought, had she sent him here, to the orphanage?

"Yes, roller skates. I let the other boys use them. They always borrow them. But they're careful of them."

What reason other than poverty—?

"I'm going to take the money you gave me for taking care of Pat," he said, "and buy her a pair of gloves."

I could only say, "That will be nice. Do you know her size?"

"I think it's 8½," he said.

He looked at my hands.

"Do you wear 8½?" he asked.

"No. I wear a smaller size, a 6."

"Oh! Then I guess her hands are bigger than yours."

I hated her, poverty or not! The soul could starve as quickly as the body. He was buying gloves for her, and she lived away from him in Mannville, and was content to send him skates!

I decided that I should not leave without seeing her and knowing for myself why she had done this thing.

But the mind scatters its interests, and I did not take time to go to Mannville, or even to speak to the orphanage officials about her. And after my first fury at her, we did not speak of her again.

He came every day and cut my wood and did small helpful favors and stayed to talk. The days had become cold, and often I let him come inside the cabin. He would lie on the floor in front of the fire, with one arm across the dog, and they would both doze and wait quietly for me. Other days, they ran together through the woods. Finally, I was ready to go.

I said to him, "You have been my good friend, Jerry. I shall often think of you and miss you. I am leaving tomorrow."

He did not answer. When he went away, I remember that a new moon hung over the mountains. I watched him go in silence up the hill. I expected him the next day, but he did not come. The details of packing occupied me until late in the day. I closed the cabin and started the car, noticing that the sun was in the west and that I would be lucky to be out of the mountains by nightfall. I stopped by the orphanage and left the cabin key with Miss Clark.

"And will you call Jerry for me to say goodbye to him?"

"I don't know where he is," she said. "I'm afraid he's not well. He didn't eat his dinner this noon. It's not like him."

I was almost relieved, for I knew I should never see him again, and it would be easier not to say goodbye to him.

I said, "I wanted to talk to you about his mother—about why he's here. But I'm in more of a hurry than I expected to be. It's out of the question for me to see her now too. But here's some money I'd like to leave with you to buy things for him at Christmas and on his birthday. It will be better than trying to send him things. I could so easily send something he has—skates, for instance."

She blinked her eyes.

"There's not much use for skates here," she said.

Her stupidity annoyed me.

"What I mean," I said, "is that I don't want to duplicate things his mother sends him. I might have chosen skates if I didn't know she had already given them to him."

She stared at me.

"I don't understand," she said. "He has no mother. He has no skates."

TELLING ABOUT THE STORY. Complete each of the following statements by putting an *x* in the box next to the correct answer. Each statement tells something about the story.

1. At the beginning of the story, the writer thought that Jerry
   - ☐ a. would not get along with her dog.
   - ☐ b. would not be willing to work for her.
   - ☐ c. was too small to chop wood well.

2. When the writer was delayed by fog, Jerry
   - ☐ a. fed and cared for the dog.
   - ☐ b. made a place near the fireplace to store wood.
   - ☐ c. did some work on the path near the cabin.

3. Jerry told the writer that he was planning to
   - ☐ a. leave the orphanage soon.
   - ☐ b. give her a present.
   - ☐ c. buy a pair of gloves for his mother.

4. Miss Clark informed the writer that Jerry
   - ☐ a. was feeling very well.
   - ☐ b. already had some skates.
   - ☐ c. had no mother.

WATCHING FOR NEW VOCABULARY WORDS. Answer the following vocabulary questions by putting an *x* in the box next to the correct response.

1. According to the writer, Jerry was more than honest—he had integrity. Which expression best defines the word *integrity?*
   - ☐ a. being truthful and sincere
   - ☐ b. being false and untrue
   - ☐ c. possessing great riches

2. The writer stated that she did not wish to duplicate things Jerry's mother had given him—skates, for example. As used in this sentence, the word *duplicate* means
   - ☐ a. sell.
   - ☐ b. borrow.
   - ☐ c. repeat.

3. Jerry said that he would split kindling, as well as medium wood and some large logs. What is the meaning of the word *kindling?*
   - ☐ a. large stones used for making a path
   - ☐ b. small pieces of wood for starting a fire
   - ☐ c. kind and thoughtful acts

4. Fog filled the mountains so treacherously that it was unsafe to drive. What is the meaning of the word *treacherously?*
   - ☐ a. clearly
   - ☐ b. dangerously
   - ☐ c. sharply

☐ × 5 = ☐

NUMBER CORRECT   YOUR SCORE

☐ × 5 = ☐

NUMBER CORRECT   YOUR SCORE

IDENTIFYING STORY ELEMENTS. Each of the following questions tests your understanding of story elements. Put an *x* in the box next to each correct answer.

1. Where is "A Mother in Mannville" *set?*
   - ☐ a. in a camp for boys
   - ☐ b. in a cabin in the Carolina mountains
   - ☐ c. on a farm

2. Identify the group of words which best *characterizes* Jerry?
   - ☐ a. thoughtful, gracious, hardworking
   - ☐ b. lazy, careless, clumsy
   - ☐ c. tall, well dressed, powerful

3. Which line of *dialogue* by Jerry affected the writer most deeply?
   - ☐ a. Size don't matter chopping wood.
   - ☐ b. I told them I thought you would want to see me.
   - ☐ c. My mother lives in Mannville.

4. What happened last in the *plot* of the story?
   - ☐ a. The writer stopped by the orphanage to leave a key with Miss Clark.
   - ☐ b. Jerry told the writer that she looked like his mother.
   - ☐ c. Jerry chopped an astonishing amount of wood.

SELECTING WORDS FROM THE STORY. Complete the following paragraph by filling in each blank with one of the words listed below. Each of the words appears in the story. Since there are five words and four blanks, one word in the group will not be used.

Marjorie Kinnan Rawlings, the author of "A Mother in Mannville," lived in Florida for many _____ . It is the setting for most of her _____ . *The Yearling,* Rawlings's most famous novel, takes _____ in the backwoods of Florida. This _____ story of a boy who adopts an orphaned deer won a Pulitzer Prize in 1939.

writing   cabin

place

years   splendid

☐ × 5 = ☐

NUMBER CORRECT   YOUR SCORE

☐ × 5 = ☐

NUMBER CORRECT   YOUR SCORE

THINKING ABOUT THE STORY. Each of the following questions requires you to think critically about the selection. Put an *x* in the box next to the correct answer.

1. We may infer that the writer
   ☐ a. did not care much about Jerry.
   ☐ b. grew very fond of Jerry.
   ☐ c. eventually found Jerry's mother.

2. On the day that the writer left, Jerry felt ill and didn't eat his dinner. Probably, he felt sick because he
   ☐ a. had eaten something that did not agree with him.
   ☐ b. had worked too hard earlier that day.
   ☐ c. was very upset that the writer was leaving.

3. At the end of the story, both the writer and Miss Clark were
   ☐ a. surprised.
   ☐ b. pleased.
   ☐ c. saddened.

4. Possibly, Jerry said he had a mother in Mannville because he
   ☐ a. felt sorry for the writer.
   ☐ b. wanted a mother so badly that he created one.
   ☐ c. he wanted to live in Mannville.

Thinking More About the Story

- Suppose that Jerry had found words to express his feelings to the writer just before she left. What do you think Jerry would have said to her?
- The writer's dog, Pat, plays an important role in "A Mother in Mannville." Using examples from the story, support this statement.
- According to the writer, Jerry was unusually honest. At the end of the story, however, we discover that Jerry was not always truthful. What things did Jerry tell the writer which were not true? Why do you think he said these things?

Use the boxes below to total your scores for the exercises.

☐
+
Telling About the Story

☐
+
Watching for New Vocabulary Words

☐
+
Identifying Story Elements

☐
+
Selecting Words from the Story

☐
▼
Thinking About the Story

☐
Score Total: Story 15

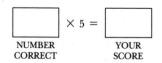

☐ × 5 = ☐

NUMBER   YOUR
CORRECT   SCORE

16. Clothes Make the Man

by Henri Duvernois

I don't like it," Tango complained again. "I won't feel right, walking up and down in that."

"Shut up and put it on," Mireault told him, and so, of course, Tango obeyed. Mireault was half his size but he was clever. If they had given Tango a tail, he would have put it between his legs when Mireault spoke.

"Now, see?" Mireault said. "What did I tell you? Looks good, doesn't it? See, you've even got a whistle."

"Not bad," Tango had to admit, looking at himself in the mirror. He pushed out his mighty chest and threw back his broad shoulders. Even the Eel, the quick silent one who was Mireault's working partner and who rarely opened his mouth, was stirred to speech. "Boy, ain't he handsome!" he said.

No question about it, Tango made a noble sight. The policeman's uniform might have been made for him by the best tailor in Paris. His little eyes looked brighter under the visor of the jaunty cap; they almost looked intelligent.

"Stop gawking at yourself and wipe that dumb grin off your face," Mireault said impatiently, "and listen. This is so simple a half-wit could do it, so maybe if you try hard you can too."

With regret Tango turned away from the mirror. His broad forehead wrinkled in the painful expression that meant he was concentrating.

"All you do is walk up and down the street," Mireault said. "Easy and slow, like a real cop on his beat. Then if anyone hears us working in the house they won't get suspicious, seeing you. Keep walking until we come out, then hang around a few minutes covering us. That's all there is to it. We'll meet back here. Now you understand?"

"Sure," Tango said, his eyes straying to the mirror.

"Then get going!" Mireault snapped.

Tango was a little nervous walking to the street Mireault and the Eel had picked out, but nothing happened. It was a well-to-do section, and in the dim glow of the shaded corner light Tango could see what fine houses they were—sober, solid, well cared for. The house where the job was to be pulled was in the middle of the block, behind a garden wall. Mireault and the Eel had cased it thoroughly; there was a tin-can wall safe upstairs with a very nice load of money inside. It seemed that the old-fashioned family didn't believe in banks. Maybe they would, Mireault had said, after tonight.

Tango wondered what it would be like to live in so fine a house, but the effort of imagination was beyond him. He had seldom ever seen a street such as this one. He worked in the shabby quarters of Paris—a little purse-snatching, a little shoplifting; he even panhandled. Yes, he was good at panhandling. Timid businessmen usually came right across when Tango's huge shoulders towered over them; they looked fearfully at the massive hands and dug for whatever change they had.

He sauntered down the pavement, turned at the corner and came back. Halfway, he saw the two shadowy figures slip over the garden wall and disappear. Mireault and the Eel were at work.

Tango fell to thinking of how he had looked in the mirror. With the impressive sight vivid in his mind, he straightened his shoulders and threw out his chest again. Standing tall, he tried a salute. It felt good. He grinned, oddly pleased, and walked on.

It was while he was turning at the other corner that he saw the police lieutenant.

Such a sight was usually enough to send him traveling as fast as his feet would move. He stared in horror. He fancied that the lieutenant, getting closer, was looking at him curiously. Tango's body was rigid; his palms were sweating. With a tremendous effort he held down the wild impulse to dash away. He shuddered. Then, stiffly, with the policeman no more than a few feet from him, he raised his arm and saluted.

The policeman casually returned the salute and passed by.

Tango stood looking after him. After a moment, he felt an odd gratification. "Say!" he said to himself. "Say, you see that? I salute, and he salutes right back. Say, that—that's pretty fine!"

It was extraordinary, the pleasure it gave him. He almost wanted to run up to the lieutenant and salute again. He threw back his shoulders straighter than ever and, erect and proud, walked down the pavement. At the corner he paused and rocked on his heels a moment as all policemen do.

"I guess I looked good to him," he told himself. "I guess he don't see many cops looking so good."

After a few more trips, he found an old lady hesitating on the corner. He saw her make two or three false starts to get across and each time nervously come back.

Tango did not even notice the fat-looking purse in her hand. He stepped in front of her, saluted, and offered his arm. She looked at him with a sweet smile. "Oh, thank you, officer!" she said.

There was no traffic in sight, but Tango held up his other arm majestically, as if stopping a horde of roaring trucks. With great dignity they crossed to the other side. It was a pretty picture indeed.

"Thank you so much, officer!" she said.

"Please madam," Tango said, "don't mention it." He paused. "That's what we're here for, you know," he added. And, gallantly, he saluted again.

He stood proudly watching her retreating figure. Before she had quite disappeared, she glanced back to give him another smile. Tango stood so straight the cloth strained across his chest. With a flourish, he saluted once more.

He went down the block, saluting at intervals. A strange feeling was stirring in him. In all Paris there could have been no more perfect an example of the calm, strong, resourceful guardian of law and order.

A disheveled figure came weaving toward him out of the shadows. It was a man, waving his arms aggressively, shuffling his feet and muttering savage but unintelligible curses. His glazed eyes fell upon Tango and he scowled. "Yea!" he cried. "Rotten cop!"

A deep sense of shock ran through Tango. "Here! Here!" he said. "Get along, get along."

"Big cowardly cop!" the drunk yelled. "Big bag of wind in a uniform! Beat up the little fellow and let the big crooks go! Thass all y'good for—beat up the little fellows an'—"

A mixed emotion of outrage and anger grew in Tango. A flush rose to his face.

."I spit on you!" the drunk declared scornfully. "Bah! There!" And he fit the action to the words.

Something popped in Tango's head. His face was purple. He grabbed the other with one mighty hand, shook him ferociously, and without any clear idea of what he was going to do with him, dragged him off the street.

Frightened, shaken out of his wits, the drunk was now passive and silent. But Tango was beside himself, and when, halfway down the block, two figures came gliding over the garden wall and landed on the pavement near him, he was in no mood to stop.

"You fool, what are you doing?" Mireault said in a furious whisper. "You want to blow the whole job? Let go of him, Blockhead!" And he struck Tango across the cheek.

Indescribable emotions swirled in Tango's head. He remembered the lieutenant answering his salute. He remembered the old lady's look of admiring gratitude. He remembered the splendid figure of himself in the mirror. And he remembered what the drunk had said.

He arose to the full pitch of a mighty fury. While Mireault and the Eel stared at him in open-mouthed horror, he stuffed the shiny whistle in his mouth and blew several blasts loud and long enough to bring all the police in Paris.

"Crooks, robbers!" he bellowed. "I arrest you! I arrest you in the name of the law!"

TELLING ABOUT THE STORY. Complete each of the following statements by putting an *x* in the box next to the correct answer. Each statement tells something about the story.

1. Mireault and the Eel were planning to
   - ☐ a. steal a purse.
   - ☐ b. rob a safe full of money.
   - ☐ c. shoplift something from a store.

2. Tango's job was to
   - ☐ a. walk up and down the street, pretending to be a policeman.
   - ☐ b. arrest anyone who tried to break the law.
   - ☐ c. make friends with the other policemen in the area.

3. The drunk accused Tango of
   - ☐ a. being a member of a gang of crooks.
   - ☐ b. making believe that he was a police officer.
   - ☐ c. picking on the little fellow and letting the big crooks go.

4. Mireault and the Eel stared at Tango in horror when he
   - ☐ a. saluted the police lieutenant.
   - ☐ b. blew several loud blasts on his whistle.
   - ☐ c. helped an elderly lady across the street.

WATCHING FOR NEW VOCABULARY WORDS. Answer the following vocabulary questions by putting an *x* in the box next to the correct response.

1. Tango had broad shoulders, a mighty chest, and massive hands. What is the meaning of the word *massive?*
   - ☐ a. long and slender
   - ☐ b. weak and lacking power
   - ☐ c. large and bulky

2. In a policeman's uniform, Tango looked very handsome; he certainly was an impressive sight. The word *impressive* means
   - ☐ a. striking or splendid.
   - ☐ b. forgettable or unimportant.
   - ☐ c. silly or foolish.

3. Frightened out of his wits, the man became passive and quiet. Select the expression which best defines the word *passive.*
   - ☐ a. loud and noisy
   - ☐ b. peaceful and yielding
   - ☐ c. dangerous and harmful

4. With one hand Tango shook the man ferociously, then dragged him off the street. The word *ferociously* means
   - ☐ a. gently.
   - ☐ b. fiercely.
   - ☐ c. cheerfully.

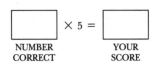

☐ × 5 = ☐

NUMBER CORRECT   YOUR SCORE

☐ × 5 = ☐

NUMBER CORRECT   YOUR SCORE

115

IDENTIFYING STORY ELEMENTS. Each of the following questions tests your understanding of story elements. Put an *x* in the box next to each correct answer.

1. Where is "Clothes Make the Man" *set?*
   ☐ a. on the streets of Paris
   ☐ b. in the back alleys of Paris
   ☐ c. in a police station in Paris

2. Identify the statement which *characterizes* the way Tango changed.
   ☐ a. At first he was an enemy of the law; later he became the law's friend.
   ☐ b. At first he disliked Mireault and the Eel; later he admired them.
   ☐ c. At first he was a follower in the gang; later he became its leader.

3. Which one of the following statements *foreshadows* the ending of the story?
   ☐ a. Tango saw the two shadowy figures slip over the garden wall and disappear.
   ☐ b. A strange feeling was stirring in Tango. In all Paris there could have been no more perfect an example of law and order.
   ☐ c. Tango wondered what it would be like to live in so fine a house.

4. What happened last in the *plot?*
   ☐ a. A policeman saluted Tango.
   ☐ b. A man accused Tango of being a rotten cop.
   ☐ c. Tango attempted to arrest Mireault and the Eel.

☐ × 5 = ☐

NUMBER CORRECT   YOUR SCORE

SELECTING WORDS FROM THE STORY. Complete the following paragraph by filling in each blank with one of the words listed below. Each of the words appears in the story. Since there are five words and four blanks, one word in the group will not be used.

In France, police _____ are called
                          1
gendarmes. In their blue uniforms and peaked

caps, they are a familiar _____ . You
                                 2
can see them guarding important buildings,

directing _____ , and providing
              3
protection to the citizens of the country.

There are _____ than 60,000 police
                4
officers in France. The city of Paris is so large,

it has its own police force.

partner   traffic

sight

more   officers

☐ × 5 = ☐

NUMBER CORRECT   YOUR SCORE

THINKING ABOUT THE STORY. Each of the following questions requires you to think critically about the selection. Put an *x* in the box next to the correct answer.

1. Tango's experiences while he was wearing a policeman's uniform made him feel
   □ a. frightened.
   □ b. sad.
   □ c. proud.

2. The last two paragraphs of the story hint that Mireault and the Eel probably
   □ a. escaped with the stolen money.
   □ b. were captured by the police.
   □ c. tried to attack Tango.

3. Clues in the story suggest that Tango
   □ a. was sorry he let his friends down.
   □ b. will certainly return to a life of crime.
   □ c. had the makings of a fine policeman.

4. Select the sentence which expresses a point this story makes.
   □ a. How we view ourselves can strongly affect our actions.
   □ b. It is usually possible to correctly guess how an acquaintance will act.
   □ c. A person who was once a criminal will always remain a criminal.

	× 5 =	
NUMBER CORRECT		YOUR SCORE

Thinking More About the Story

● At the beginning of the story, Tango complained that he wouldn't "feel right" walking up and down in a policeman's uniform. Did this prove to be the case? Explain.

● Immediately before he blew the police whistle, Tango remembered several things: the lieutenant answering his salute, the old lady's admiring look, the splendid figure of himself in the mirror, and the words the drunk had said. Show how each of these contributed to Tango's blowing the whistle.

● Why is this story called "Clothes Make the Man"? Do you think it is a good title for the selection? Explain.

Use the boxes below to total your scores for the exercises.

	Telling About the Story
+	
	Watching for New Vocabulary Words
+	
	Identifying Story Elements
+	
	Selecting Words from the Story
+	
	Thinking About the Story
▼	
	Score Total: Story 16

117

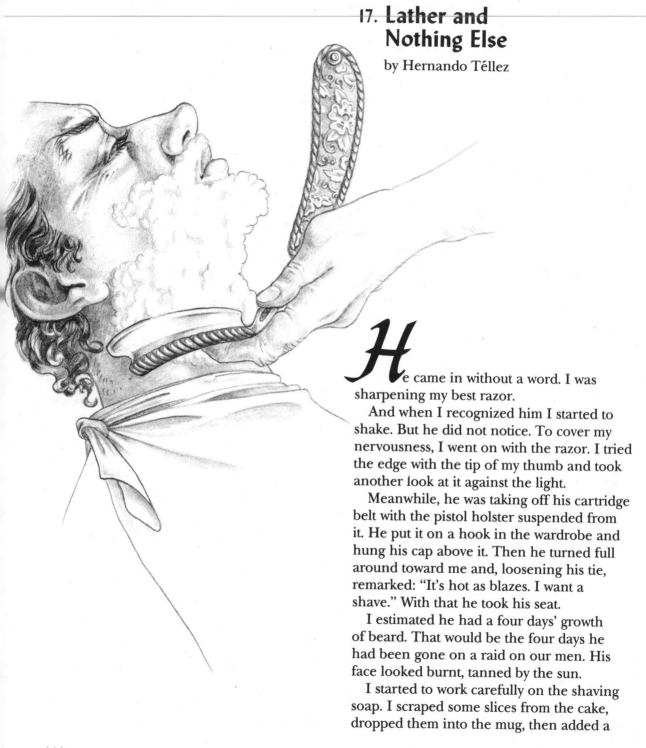

17. Lather and Nothing Else

by Hernando Téllez

*H*e came in without a word. I was sharpening my best razor.

And when I recognized him I started to shake. But he did not notice. To cover my nervousness, I went on with the razor. I tried the edge with the tip of my thumb and took another look at it against the light.

Meanwhile, he was taking off his cartridge belt with the pistol holster suspended from it. He put it on a hook in the wardrobe and hung his cap above it. Then he turned full around toward me and, loosening his tie, remarked: "It's hot as blazes. I want a shave." With that he took his seat.

I estimated he had a four days' growth of beard. That would be the four days he had been gone on a raid on our men. His face looked burnt, tanned by the sun.

I started to work carefully on the shaving soap. I scraped some slices from the cake, dropped them into the mug, then added a little lukewarm water, and stirred with the brush. The lather soon began to rise.

"We were gone long enough to get a good start on a beard," he said. I went on stirring up the lather.

"It was a good outing," he continued. "We caught the leaders. Some of them we brought back dead. Others are still alive. But they'll all be dead soon."

"How many did you take?" I asked.

"Fourteen. We had to go pretty far in to find them. But now they're paying for it. And not one will escape. Not a single one."

He leaned back in the chair when he saw the brush in my hand, full of lather. I had not yet put the sheet on him. I was certainly flustered. Taking a sheet from the drawer, I tied it around this villain's neck.

He went on talking. He evidently took it for granted I was on the side of the existing government.

"The people must have gotten a scare with what happened the other day," he said.

"Yes," I replied, as I finished tying the knot on the back of his neck, which smelled of sweat.

"Good show, wasn't it?"

"Very good," I answered, turning my attention now to the brush. The man closed his eyes wearily and awaited the cool caress of the lather.

I had never seen him so close before. The day he ordered the people to file through the schoolyard to look upon the four rebels hanging there, my path had crossed his briefly. But the sight of those mutilated bodies kept me from paying attention to the face of the man who had been directing it all. And here he was now—I had him in my hands.

It was not a disagreeable face, certainly. And the beard, which aged him a bit, was not unbecoming. His name was Torres, Captain Torres.

I started to put on the first coat of lather. He kept his eyes closed.

"I would love to catch a nap," he said, "but there's a lot to be done this evening."

I lifted the brush and asked, "A firing squad?"

"Something of the sort," he replied.

"All of them?"

"No, just a few."

I went on lathering his face. My hands began to tremble again. The man could not be aware of this, which was lucky for me. But I wished he had not come in. Probably many of our men had seen him enter the shop. And with the enemy in my house I felt a certain responsibility.

I would have to shave his beard just as I would for anyone else. I would have to be careful and neat, as if he were a regular customer. I would have to take care not to make even the tiniest nick in the skin of his face and neck. I would have to see to it that the blade did not slip. I would have to leave the skin clean, soft, shining, so that when I passed the back of my hand over it not a single hair could be felt. Yes. I was secretly a revolutionary, but at the same time I was a conscientious barber, proud of the way I did my job. And that four-day beard presented a challenge.

I took up the razor, opened the handle wide to release the blade, and started to work downward from one sideburn. The blade responded to perfection. The hair was thick. Little by little the skin began to show through. The razor gave out its usual sound as it gathered up layers of soap mixed with bits of hair. I paused to wipe it clean. Then I went about sharpening the blade again, for I am, as I say, a very careful barber.

His face was now almost entirely clean-shaven. He looked younger, several years younger than when he had come in. I suppose that always happens to men who enter and leave barbershops. Under the strokes of my razor, Torres was made young again. Yes, because I am a good barber, the best in this town, and I say this in all modesty.

A little more lather here under the chin, on the Adam's apple, right near the great vein. How hot it is! Torres must be sweating just as I am. But he is not afraid. He is perfectly relaxed, not even giving thought to what he will do to his prisoners this evening. I, on the other hand, I who am cleaning his skin with this razor, carefully avoiding the drawing of blood, careful with every stroke—I cannot keep my thoughts in order.

Blast the moment he entered my shop! I am a revolutionary but not a murderer. And it would be so easy to kill him. He deserves it. Or does he? No. No one deserves to be sacrificed because someone else wishes to be an assassin. What is to be gained by it? Nothing. Others and still others keep coming. The first kills the second, and then these kill the next, and so on until everything becomes a sea of blood. I could cut his throat—swish, swish! With his eyes shut he would not even see the flash of the razor or the gleam in my eye. He would not even have time to moan.

I'm sure that with a good strong blow, a deep cut, he would feel no pain. He would not suffer at all. And what would I do then with the body? Where would I hide it? I would have to flee, leave all this behind, take shelter far away, very far away. But they would follow until they caught up with me. "The murderer of Captain Torres. He slit his throat while he was shaving him. What a cowardly thing to do!"

And others would say: "The avenger of our people! A name to remember! He was the town barber. No one knew he was fighting for our cause."

The man, who had kept his eyes closed, now opened them, put a hand out from under the sheet, felt the part of his face which had been shaved, and said: "Come at six o'clock this evening to the school."

"Will it be like the other day?" I asked, stiff with horror.

"It may be even better," he replied.

"What are you planning to do?"

"I'm not sure yet. But we'll have a good time."

"Once more he leaned back and shut his eyes. I came closer, the razor held high.

"Are you going to punish all of them?" I timidly ventured.

"Yes, all of them."

The lather was drying on his face. I must hurry. Through the mirror, I took a look at the street. It appeared about as usual. There was the grocery shop with two or three customers. Then I glanced at the clock—two-thirty.

The razor kept moving—up, down, up, down. Now from the other sideburn, up, down. It was a blue beard, a thick one. He should let it grow like some poets, or some priests. It would suit him well. Many people would not recognize him. And that would be a good thing for him, I thought, as I went gently over all the throat line. At this point you really have to handle your blade skillfully. Here at the throat the pores of the skin might open, allowing tiny drops of blood to emerge. A good barber like myself stakes his reputation on not permitting this to happen to any of his customers.

And this was indeed a special customer. How many of ours had he sent to their deaths? How many had he had mutilated? It was best not to think about it. Torres did not know I was his enemy. Neither he nor the others knew it. It was a secret shared by very few, which made it possible for me to inform the revolutionaries about Torres's activities in the town, to tell them what he planned to do when he went on one of his raids to hunt down rebels. So it was going to be very difficult to explain how it was that I had him in my hands and then let him go in peace, alive, clean-shaven.

And so, which will it be? Murderer or hero? My fate hangs on the edge of this razor blade. I can turn my wrist slightly, put a bit more pressure on the blade, let it sink in. The skin will yield like silk—oh, so easy!

There is nothing more tender than human skin. A razor like this cannot fail. It is the best one I have.

But I don't want to be a murderer. No! The man came in to be shaved. And I do my work honorably. I don't want to stain my hands with blood. Just with lather, and nothing else. You are an executioner. I am only a barber. Each one to his job. That's it—each one to his job.

The chin was now clean, polished, soft. Torres got up and looked at himself in the glass. He ran his hand over the skin and felt its freshness, its newness.

"Thanks," he said.

He walked to the wardrobe for his belt, his gun, and his cap. I must have been very pale, and I felt my shirt soaked with sweat. He adjusted his belt buckle and straightened his gun in its holster. He smoothed his hair and put on his cap. Then, from his pants pocket, he took some coins, paid for his shave, and went to the door. There he stopped for a moment and turned toward me.

"They told me you would kill me," he said. "I came to find out if it was true. But it's not easy to kill. I know what I'm talking about."

TELLING ABOUT THE STORY. Complete each of the following statements by putting an *x* in the box next to the correct answer. Each statement tells something about the story.

1. When the barber realized that it was Captain Torres who had entered his shop, he
   ☐ a. felt sorry for himself.
   ☐ b. grew very nervous.
   ☐ c. was delighted.

2. According to Captain Torres, he planned to
   ☐ a. free some enemies later that day.
   ☐ b. punish some enemies at six o'clock that evening.
   ☐ c. make peace with some enemies the next day.

3. After much thought, the barber finally decided to
   ☐ a. murder Captain Torres.
   ☐ b. conceal the fact that Captain Torres had been there.
   ☐ c. give Captain Torres a very good shave.

4. At the end of the story, Captain Torres stated that
   ☐ a. he was not happy with the shave.
   ☐ b. he was afraid of the barber.
   ☐ c. it's not easy to kill.

WATCHING FOR NEW VOCABULARY WORDS. Answer the following vocabulary questions by putting an *x* in the box next to the correct response.

1. He was a conscientious barber, proud of the way he did his work. The word *conscientious* means
   ☐ a. very careless.
   ☐ b. very careful.
   ☐ c. very wealthy.

2. The barber decided that no one deserved to be killed because someone else wished to be an assassin. Define the word *assassin*.
   ☐ a. murderer
   ☐ b. nuisance
   ☐ c. rebel

3. The barber remembered seeing the torn and mutilated bodies of the rebels. What is the meaning of the word *mutilated*?
   ☐ a. healthy
   ☐ b. broken
   ☐ c. fascinating

4. The very skillful barber handled his razor with perfection. The word *perfection* means
   ☐ a. slowly or hesitantly.
   ☐ b. fearfully or anxiously.
   ☐ c. faultlessly or excellently.

☐ × 5 = ☐
NUMBER CORRECT   YOUR SCORE

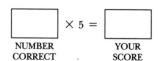
NUMBER CORRECT   YOUR SCORE

IDENTIFYING STORY ELEMENTS. Each of the following questions tests your understanding of story elements. Put an *x* in the box next to each correct answer.

1. Who is the *narrator* of "Lather and Nothing Else"?
   - ☐ a. the barber
   - ☐ b. Captain Torres
   - ☐ c. the author

2. According to Captain Torres, his *motive* for going to the barber shop was to
   - ☐ a. get a haircut.
   - ☐ b. arrest the barber.
   - ☐ c. see if the barber would kill him.

3. The barber had an *inner conflict* because he wanted to kill Captain Torres, but
   - ☐ a. did not know how to do it.
   - ☐ b. was afraid of being caught.
   - ☐ c. could not bring himself to do it.

4. Which statement best expresses the *theme* of this story?
   - ☐ a. A man's conscience proves more powerful than his desire for revenge.
   - ☐ b. A barber decides to gain revenge on an enemy.
   - ☐ c. A captain risks his life for no reason.

SELECTING WORDS FROM THE STORY. Complete the following paragraph by filling in each blank with one of the words listed below. Each of the words appears in the story. Since there are five words and four blanks, one word in the group will not be used.

Through the ages there have always been barbers. Barbers' tools such as _____ have been found in ancient Egyptian and Roman ruins. In fact, the _____ barber comes from the Latin word *barba* which means "beard." Alexander the Great ordered that his soldiers be _____ . He wanted to make sure that the enemy could not _____ them by the hair on their faces.

name   **razors**

thumb

catch   **shaved**

☐ × 5 = ☐

NUMBER CORRECT   YOUR SCORE

☐ × 5 = ☐

NUMBER CORRECT   YOUR SCORE

THINKING ABOUT THE STORY. Each of the following questions requires you to think critically about the selection. Put an *x* in the box next to the correct answer.

1. We may infer that Captain Torres knew all along that the barber
   ☐ a. believed in the existing government.
   ☐ b. was an enemy.
   ☐ c. would make him look younger.

2. At the conclusion of the story, the barber must have realized that Captain Torres
   ☐ a. was going to put him in jail.
   ☐ b. was going to become a regular customer.
   ☐ c. knew he was a revolutionary.

3. It is reasonable to conclude that Captain Torres was
   ☐ a. brave.
   ☐ b. cowardly.
   ☐ c. weak.

4. Torres's last words suggest that he
   ☐ a. seldom thought about his work.
   ☐ b. always enjoyed his work.
   ☐ c. sometimes found his work painful.

Thinking More About the Story

● The barber had to decide whether or not to kill Captain Torres. What reasons did the barber have for killing Torres? What reasons did he give for *not* killing him?
● Review your answers to the questions above. Do you think the barber made the right decision? Explain your answer.
● Why is this story called "Lather and Nothing Else"? Do you think it is a good title for the selection? Explain.

Use the boxes below to total your scores for the exercises.

☐ + **T**elling About the Story

☐ + **W**atching for New Vocabulary Words

☐ + **I**dentifying Story Elements

☐ + **S**electing Words from the Story

☐ ▼ **T**hinking About the Story

☐ **S**core Total: Story 17

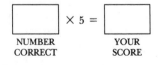

☐ × 5 = ☐
NUMBER   YOUR
CORRECT   SCORE

18. Test

by Theodore Thomas

Robert Proctor was a good driver for so young a man. The Turnpike curved gently ahead of him. There was not much traffic on this cool morning in May. He felt relaxed and alert. Two hours of driving had produced no twinges of fatigue in him. The sun was bright but not glaring, and the air smelled fresh and clean. He breathed it deeply, and blew it out noisily. It was a good day for driving.

He glanced quickly at the slim, gray-haired woman who was sitting in the front seat with him. Her mouth was curved in a quiet smile. She watched the trees and the fields slip by on her side of the Turnpike. Robert Proctor immediately looked back at the road. He said, "Enjoying it, Mom?"

125

"Yes, Robert." Her voice was as cool as the morning. "It is very pleasant to sit here," she said. "I was thinking of the driving I did for you when you were little. I wonder if you enjoyed it as much as I enjoy this."

He smiled, embarrassed. "Sure I did."

She reached over and patted him gently on the arm and then turned back to the scenery.

He listened to the smooth purr of the engine. Up ahead he saw a large truck spouting clouds of smoke as it sped along the Turnpike. Behind it, not passing it, was a long blue convertible, content to drive in the shadow of the truck.

Robert Proctor noted the arrangement and filed it in the back of his mind. He was slowly overtaking them, but he would not reach them for another minute or two.

He listened to the purr of the engine, and he was pleased with the sound. He had tuned that engine himself despite the objections of the mechanic. The engine idled roughly now, but it ran smoothly at high speed. You had to have a special touch to do good work on engines, and Robert Proctor knew he had it. No one in the world had a touch like his for the tune of an engine.

It was a good morning for driving, and his mind was filled with good thoughts. He pulled nearly alongside the blue convertible and began to pass it. His speed was a few miles per hour above the Turnpike limit, but his car was under perfect control.

The blue convertible suddenly swung out from behind the truck. It swung out without warning and struck his car near the right front fender, knocking his car to the shoulder on the left side of the Turnpike lane.

Robert Proctor was a good driver. He was too wise to slam on the brakes. He fought the steering wheel to keep the car on a straight path. The left wheels sank into the soft left shoulder, and the car tugged, pulling to the left, heading across the island toward the lanes carrying the cars in the opposite direction. Then a wheel struck a rock buried in the soft dirt. The left front tire blew out and the car spun wildly. It was then that his mother began to scream.

The car turned sideways and skidded part of the way into the other lanes. Robert Proctor fought against the steering wheel, trying to straighten the car. But the drag of the blown tire was too much.

His mother's scream rang steadily in his ears. And even as he strained at the wheel, one part of his mind coolly wondered how a single scream could last so long. Then an oncoming car struck his radiator from the side and spun him viciously into the middle of the left-hand lanes.

He was flung against his mother's lap, and she was thrown against the right-hand door. It held. With his left hand he reached for the steering wheel. He pulled himself erect, fighting the force of the spin. He turned the wheel to the left and tried to stop the spin, to get out of the lanes of oncoming traffic.

The car lost some of its momentum. During one of the spins he twisted the wheel straight. The car, wobbling, stopped spinning and headed down the lane. But before Robert Proctor could turn it off the Turnpike to safety, a car loomed ahead of him. It was bearing down on him.

There was a man at the wheel of that

other car. He was sitting rigid, unable to move, eyes wide and staring and filled with fright. Alongside the man was a girl. Her head was against the back of the seat, her eyes closed in peaceful sleep.

It was not the fear in the man that touched Robert Proctor. It was the trusting helplessness in the face of the sleeping girl. The two cars sped closer to each other, and Robert Proctor could not change the direction of his car. The driver of the other car remained frozen at the wheel.

Robert Proctor sat motionless, staring into the face of the onrushing sleeping girl. His mother's cry still sounded in his ears. He heard no crash when the two cars collided head-on at a high rate of speed. He felt something push into his stomach, and the world began to go gray. Just before he lost consciousness, he heard the scream stop. He knew then that he had been hearing a single, short scream that had only seemed to drag on and on. Then there came darkness.

Robert Proctor seemed to be at the bottom of a deep black well. There was a spot of light in the far distance, and he could hear the rumble of a distant voice. He tried to pull himself toward the light and the sound, but the effort was too great. He lay still and gathered himself and tried again. The light grew brighter and the voice louder. He tried harder, again, and he drew closer. Then he opened his eyes fully and looked at the man sitting in front of him.

"You all right, Son?" asked the man. He wore a blue uniform, and his round, beefy face was familiar.

Robert Proctor slowly moved his head. He discovered that he was seated, unharmed, in a reclining chair, and was able to move his arms and legs with no trouble. He looked around the room, and he remembered.

The man in the uniform saw the growing intelligence in Robert Proctor's eyes and he said, "No harm done, Son. You just took the last part of your driver's test."

Robert Proctor focused his eyes on the man. Though he saw the man clearly, he seemed to see the faint face of the sleeping girl in front of him.

The uniformed man continued to speak. "We put you into a deep sleep and then put you through an accident under hypnosis. We do it to everybody these days before they get their driver's licenses. It makes better drivers of them, more careful drivers for the rest of their lives. Do you remember it now? Remember coming in here and all?"

Robert Proctor nodded. He was thinking of his mother and of the sleeping girl. She would never have awakened. She would have passed right from a sweet, temporary sleep into the dark, heavy sleep of death.

The uniformed man was still speaking. "So you're all set now. You pay me the ten dollar fee, and sign this application. We'll have your license in the mail in a day or two." The man did not look up.

Robert Proctor placed a ten dollar bill on the table in front of him. He glanced over the application and signed it. He looked up to find two men in white uniforms standing there, one on each side of him. Robert Proctor frowned in annoyance and started to speak. But the uniformed man spoke first.

"Sorry, Son. You failed. You're sick. You need treatment."

The two men helped Robert Proctor to his feet, and he said, "Take your hands off me. What is this?"

The uniformed man said, "Nobody should want to drive a car after going through what you just went through. It should take months before you can even think of driving again. But you're ready right now. Killing people doesn't bother you. We don't let your kind run around loose in society anymore. But don't you worry now, Son. They'll take good care of you, and they'll fix you up." He nodded to the two men, and they began to march Robert Proctor out.

At the door he spoke, and his voice was so urgent the two men paused. Robert Proctor said, "You can't really mean this. I'm still dreaming, aren't I? This is still part of the test, isn't it?"

The uniformed man said, *"How do any of us know?"* And they dragged Robert Proctor out the door, knees stiff, feet dragging, his rubber heels sliding along the two grooves worn into the floor.

TELLING ABOUT THE STORY. Complete each of the following statements by putting an *x* in the box next to the correct answer. Each statement tells something about the story.

1. Robert Proctor was traveling in a car with
   - ☐ a. his mother.
   - ☐ b. another man.
   - ☐ c. a sleeping girl.

2. The accident occurred when
   - ☐ a. Proctor went through a red light and hit a truck.
   - ☐ b. Proctor fell asleep at the wheel and went off the road.
   - ☐ c. Proctor's car was struck by another car.

3. The accident was part of
   - ☐ a. a movie that Proctor was watching.
   - ☐ b. Proctor's driving test.
   - ☐ c. an ordinary day in Proctor's life.

4. According to the man in uniform, Proctor needed treatment because
   - ☐ a. he was badly injured in the accident.
   - ☐ b. he was a very poor driver.
   - ☐ c. killing people didn't bother him.

WATCHING FOR NEW VOCABULARY WORDS. Answer the following vocabulary questions by putting an *x* in the box next to the correct response.

1. Proctor heard no crash when the two cars collided. Which expression best defines the word *collided*?
   - ☐ a. banged together violently
   - ☐ b. picked up speed
   - ☐ c. came to a halt

2. When he saw the two men, Proctor frowned in annoyance. The word *annoyance* refers to the act of being
   - ☐ a. pleased.
   - ☐ b. bothered.
   - ☐ c. surprised.

3. The girl would have passed from a temporary sleep into the heavy sleep of death. The word *temporary* means
   - ☐ a. dark and shadowy.
   - ☐ b. very chilly.
   - ☐ c. for a limited time.

4. Finally, the car slowed down as it lost some of its momentum. What is the meaning of the word *momentum*?
   - ☐ a. force
   - ☐ b. glass
   - ☐ c. fuel

☐ × 5 = ☐

NUMBER
CORRECT

YOUR
SCORE

☐ × 5 = ☐

NUMBER
CORRECT

YOUR
SCORE

IDENTIFYING STORY ELEMENTS. Each of the following questions tests your understanding of story elements. Put an *x* in the box next to each correct answer.

1. When is this story *set?*
   ☐ a. in the distant past
   ☐ b. at the present time
   ☐ c. in the future

2. Robert Proctor may be *characterized* as a young man who did not realize that
   ☐ a. he was a danger to himself and to others.
   ☐ b. it always pays to show kindness to others.
   ☐ c. his mother cared for him very much.

3. What happened last in the *plot* of the story?
   ☐ a. Robert Proctor was dragged out of the room.
   ☐ b. The two cars sped closer to each other.
   ☐ c. Robert Proctor signed the application.

4. What is the author's *purpose* in writing "Test"?
   ☐ a. to make the reader laugh
   ☐ b. to make the reader sad
   ☐ c. to teach the reader a lesson

SELECTING WORDS FROM THE STORY. Complete the following paragraph by filling in each blank with one of the words listed below. Each of the words appears in the story. Since there are five words and four blanks, one word in the group will not be used.

Here are a few driving tips to help prevent you from getting into an _____ .₁ First, don't _____₂ if you are very tired or have been drinking. About half of the highway deaths in the United States are related to alcohol. Obey the speed _____₃ and allow plenty of space between your vehicle and the one in front of you. Always wear your _____₄ belt, and keep your car in good operating condition.

accident   mechanic

limit

drive   seat

	× 5 =	
NUMBER CORRECT		YOUR SCORE

	× 5 =	
NUMBER CORRECT		YOUR SCORE

THINKING ABOUT THE STORY. Each of the following questions requires you to think critically about the selection. Put an *x* in the box next to the correct answer.

1. Robert Proctor failed the driving test because he
   - ☐ a. nearly killed two people.
   - ☐ b. didn't study enough for the test.
   - ☐ c. was not sufficiently upset about his experience.

2. It is fair to say that the test Proctor took
   - ☐ a. revealed little.
   - ☐ b. revealed important information.
   - ☐ c. consisted mainly of short answer and essay questions.

3. Proctor was dragged out of the door, his heels sliding along the two grooves worn into the floor. The grooves indicate that
   - ☐ a. many other people have been dragged out of that door.
   - ☐ b. Proctor went willingly with the uniformed men.
   - ☐ c. the building was old and dangerously in need of repair.

4. This story suggests that
   - ☐ a. driving a car is very serious and should never be taken lightly.
   - ☐ b. accidents can happen, but there's not much we can do about them.
   - ☐ c. there is no way of telling if a person will be a safe driver.

```
┌─────────┐         ┌─────────┐
│         │ × 5 =   │         │
└─────────┘         └─────────┘
 NUMBER              YOUR
 CORRECT             SCORE
```

Thinking More About the Story

- Robert Proctor took a very unusual driving test. Do you think that new drivers should be given this kind of test? Offer reasons to support your opinion.
- As a result of having failed the driving test, Robert Proctor will one day be a better person. Do you agree or disagree with this statement? Explain.
- At the end of the story Proctor asked, "This is still part of the test, isn't it?" The uniformed man answered, *"How do any of us know?"* What point is the author making?

Use the boxes below to total your scores for the exercises.

```
┌─────┐
│     │  Telling About the Story
└─────┘
  +
┌─────┐
│     │  Watching for New Vocabulary Words
└─────┘
  +
┌─────┐
│     │  Identifying Story Elements
└─────┘
  +
┌─────┐
│     │  Selecting Words from the Story
└─────┘
  +
┌─────┐
│     │  Thinking About the Story
└─────┘
  ▼
┌─────┐
│     │  Score Total: Story 18
└─────┘
```

Acknowledgments

Acknowledgment is gratefully made to the following publishers, authors, and agents for permission to reprint these works. All adaptations are by Burton Goodman.

"The Interlopers" by Saki. From the *Complete Short Stories of Saki* by H. H. Munro. Copyright © 1930, renewed © 1958 by the Viking Press, Inc. Reprinted by permission of Viking Penguin, Inc.

"The Last Leaf" by O. Henry. Reprinted by permission of Doubleday, a division of Bantam, Doubleday, Dell Publishing Group, Inc.

"Appointment with Love" by S. I. Kishor. Reprinted by permission of Lenniger-Payne Literary Agency.

"The Journey" by Charles Land. Reprinted by permission of Larry Sternig Literary Agency.

"Thank You, M'am" by Langston Hughes. Copyright © 1958 by Langston Hughes, renewed © 1986 by George Houston Bass. Reprinted by permission of Harold Ober Associates, Inc.

"Sarah Tops" by Isaac Asimov. From *Boys' Life*, February 1975. © 1975 by the Boy Scouts of America. Published by permission of the Asimov Estate care of Ralph M. Vicinanza, Ltd.

"Louisa, Please Come Home." From *Come Along With Me* by Shirley Jackson. Copyright © 1960 by Shirley Jackson. All rights reserved. Reprinted by permission of Viking Penguin, Inc.

"A Dip in the Poole" by Bill Pronzini. Reprinted by permission of the author.

"The Padre's Neighbor" by Manuela Williams Crosno. Copyright © 1987 by Manuela Williams Crosno. Reprinted by permission of the author.

"Dusk" by Saki. From the *Complete Short Stories of Saki* by H. H. Munro. Copyright © 1930, renewed © 1958 by the Viking Press, Inc. Reprinted by permission of Viking Penguin, Inc.

"The Sin of Madam Phloi" by Lilian Jackson Braun. Copyright © 1962 by Davis Publications. Reprinted by permission of the author and her agent, Blanche C. Gregory, Inc.

"The Cop and the Anthem" by O. Henry. Reprinted by permission of Doubleday, a division of Bantam, Doubleday, Dell Publishing Group, Inc.

"A Mother in Mannville." From *When the Whippoorwill* by Marjorie Kinnan Rawlings. Copyright © 1940 by Marjorie Kinnan Rawlings, renewed © 1968 by Norton Baskin. Reprinted by permission of Charles Scribner's Sons, an imprint of Macmillan Publishing Company.

"Clothes Make the Man" by Henri Duvernois. Every attempt has been made to locate the author for permission to reprint this piece.

"Lather and Nothing Else" by Hernando Téllez. Reprinted from *Américas,* bimonthly magazine published by the General Secretariat of the Organization of American States.

"Test" by Theodore Thomas. Copyright © 1961 by Mercury Press, Inc. Reprinted from *The Magazine of Fantasy and Science Fiction.*

Progress Chart

1. Write in your score for each exercise.
2. Write in your Total Score.

	T	W	I	S	T	TOTAL SCORE
Story 1						
Story 2						
Story 3						
Story 4						
Story 5						
Story 6						
Story 7						
Story 8						
Story 9						
Story 10						
Story 11						
Story 12						
Story 13						
Story 14						
Story 15						
Story 16						
Story 17						
Story 18						

Progress Graph

1. Write your Total Score in the box under the number for each passage.
2. Put an x along the line above each box to show your Total Score for that passage.
3. Make a graph of your progress by drawing a line to connect the x's.

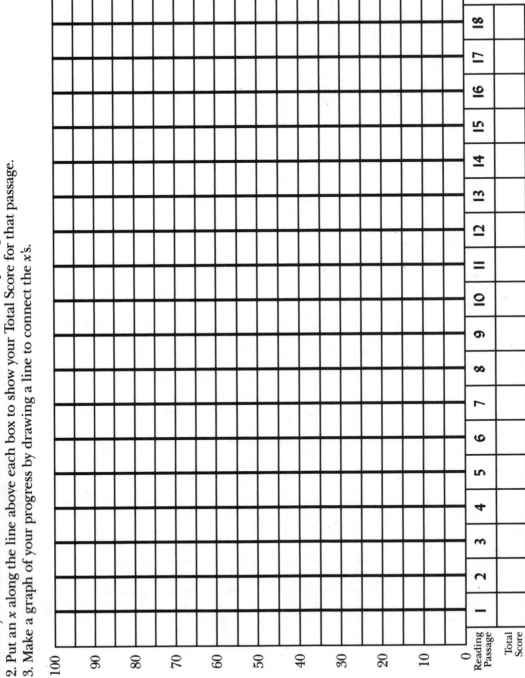

Reading Passage	1	2	3	4	5	6	7	8	9	10	11	12	13	14	15	16	17	18
Total Score																		